THE KUNG-FU DIARIES
THE LIFE AND TIMES OF
A DRAGON MASTER
(1920-2001)

FOREWORD
BY
PATRICK GRANT

The Book Guild Ltd

First published in Great Britain in 2018 by
The Book Guild Ltd
9 Priory Business Park
Wistow Road, Kibworth
Leicestershire, LE8 0RX
Freephone: 0800 999 2982
www.bookguild.co.uk
Email: info@bookguild.co.uk
Twitter: @bookguild

Copyright © 2018 Patrick Grant

The right of Patrick Grant to be identified as the author of this
work has been asserted by him in accordance with the
Copyright, Design and Patents Act 1988.

All rights reserved. No part of this publication may be
reproduced, transmitted, or stored in a retrieval system, in any form or by any means,
without permission in writing from the publisher, nor be otherwise circulated in
any form of binding or cover other than that in which it is published and without
a similar condition being imposed on the subsequent purchaser.

This work is entirely fictitious and bears no resemblance to any persons living or dead.

Typeset in Garmond

Printed and bound in Great Britain by CPI Group (UK) Ltd, Croydon, CR0 4YY

ISBN 978 1912362 370

British Library Cataloguing in Publication Data.
A catalogue record for this book is available from the British Library.

For Ed O'Brien

> "My teacher Old Shang was the strongest man in the world, yet his family knew nothing about it. He never showed his strength because he never had to use it."
>
> — Lieh Tzu

> "The virtue of a free man is as great in avoiding dangers as in overcoming them."
>
> — Benedict Spinoza

FOREWORD

The following book is not quite a biography, or a historical novel, or an adventure story, or an instructional guide. Rather, it combines these elements, among others, to provide a uniquely captivating account of what it means to be a student and practitioner of the ancient tradition of Shaolin Chan Kung-Fu. The main source material on which this account is based is a collection of diaries (actually, a boxful of assorted papers, including diaries) provided to the author by his teacher, a Kung-Fu Dragon Master. Not long before he died in 2001, the Master requested that the diaries be used as a foundation for a broadly accessible description of the 'Art', as he calls it, to which he had devoted himself throughout his life.

By asking for the book to be based on his private papers, the Master indicates that a general description of the aims and ideals of Shaolin Chan Kung-Fu would not suffice. This is so because Chan Buddhism emphasises the experience of individuals, and the Art is authentic only when it is embodied in the practice of a particular person. Yet, as we know, particular people are never perfect. And so, on the one hand, the following book presents us with a manifesto, setting out the ideals and describing the practices of an ancient wisdom tradition. On the other hand, it is shaped by a narrative that draws us, patiently and relentlessly, towards a shocking, personal act of violence and a subsequent destructive, erotic obsession that call the ideals of the manifesto radically into question. This contradiction between precept and practice, ideal and actual, lies at the heart of the Dragon Master's story.

Given the significance accorded to the Master's personal experience in the book as a whole, it might at first seem odd that both he and his student prefer to remain anonymous. Yet, their choosing to do so is entirely in keeping with the fact that Kung-Fu traditionally places a high value on self-effacement. By contrast, we might find ourselves uncomfortably reminded, here, of how far in the opposite direction the martial arts are so often taken by today's popular media. Since World War II, especially by way of export to the United States, Asian martial arts have been widely appropriated by manipulators of the marketplace and glorifiers of violence – these, as ever, being interdependent. The self-promoting antics of countless so-called experts for whom Kung-Fu is mainly a set of fighting tricks, together with the flashy exaggerations of no end of mass media 'stars', are a mere parody of what the present book presents as an authentic Kung-Fu practice.

Still, the importing of Kung-Fu and of Asian wisdom traditions in general to the West is by no means entirely negative. The writer of the diaries and his student – the editor, who also assumes a substantial authorial role in the shaping of the following book – both agree that the modern West offers special opportunities for the reception and development of Asian Taoist and Buddhist practices that were suppressed in modern China as relics of feudalism, and which indeed were all too frequently mired in superstition, faction and exploitation. And so, among other things, the following book can be read as a cross-cultural exploration, attentive to the positive outcomes of a genuine dialogue between East and West. Here, it is worth noticing that the diaries cite Sigmund Freud on more than one occasion, and, as Freud points out, the great primal drives we share most deeply as a species, across even our most pronounced cultural barriers, are

Eros and Thanatos – the life-drive and the death-drive, sex and violence. Freud argues that Eros and Thanatos should not stand opposed but should work in service of each other, and, at its core, the present book engages also with this universal drama, as the Dragon Master himself acknowledges. But what has Kung-Fu to do with Eros?

As the diaries insist, the main idea of any martial arts training worthy of serious consideration is that it brings our violent impulses more fully to consciousness, thereby enabling us better to manage them and to convert their energy to a higher, creative understanding. In so doing, the martial arts remain within the domain of Mars ('martial' has the word 'Mars' already inscribed within it), and the domain of Eros is left largely out of account. And yet there is a further, allied system of training that does for Eros exactly what martial arts training does for violence. That is, by making sexuality conscious, we can direct its energy to a higher, creative understanding in which the potential of Eros is fully realised, and where the opposition between Mars and Venus is transcended and resolved.

It is a great deal easier, of course, to set up a martial arts school in a local mall than it is to set up a school to practise the arts of Eros, which, not surprisingly, remain a closed-door teaching. Not every martial artist is likely to venture behind those closed doors, and yet every martial artist will certainly be faced with the challenges of Eros, which, as Freud argues, cannot safely remain separated from the compulsions of Thanatos. As the diaries repeatedly claim, if the wounds of Eros and Thanatos are not dealt with together, neither will be healed.

And so, the present book is quite unconventional, both in bringing us into a world of erotic secrets that are usually hidden from public view, and also in exploring the links between that world and the martial arts. But there is more. We are to learn also that a higher convergence of these expressions of our most primal energies – of Eros and Thanatos – occurs in the contemplative state that is the goal of Chi Gong meditation, the summation and highest fulfillment of the entire course of Kung-Fu training and practise.

By their nature, the documents on which the following book is based are fragmentary, and the author-editor selects, organises, and conflates a broad range of excerpts to develop an accessible and engaging narrative. Often, he has needed to conduct his own research to fill gaps and provide background information. His findings, however, are not always conclusive, and this is so partly because the diaries record events in Hong Kong, Montreal, Paris, London, and the United States. It is often difficult to recover details about the Dragon Master's comings and goings among these locations, especially considering the timescale of the narrative and the disruptions caused by the Second World War, the Japanese invasion of Hong Kong, and the civil war in China, all of which are relevant to the story. Given these complexities, it is not surprising that the author-editor sometimes settles for what seems probable in light of the evidence (or lack of it), and, consequently, the narrative sometimes depends on how he can best imagine the unfolding and interconnection of events. And yet, as the book as a whole shows, our stories are always to some degree incomplete, and, as we also learn, there is no single, complete, or orthodox version of the Art. Rather, Shaolin Chan Kung-Fu confirms that being human is, like the Art itself, an open-ended project, constituted and sustained by the same kind of many-sided dialogue as the book itself exemplifies.

I have not met the Master, but I am acquainted with his student, the author-editor, who has asked me to write this introduction. And so, in conclusion, I offer the foregoing remarks as a sincere and confident invitation to readers to engage with the following book in the spirit of the Art that it describes, and that the Dragon Master's story brings so vividly to life.

Patrick Grant

EDITOR'S NOTE

A book such as this presents many editorial challenges. Chief among them is the task of selecting materials to make a coherent story in keeping with the author's wishes. As I explain in the opening pages, I often conflate passages, at times running several together, sometimes selecting them from different source documents. Also, I omit a great deal that I judge to be of incidental interest, or to be too personal for publication.

Frequently, I have needed to conduct my own research to clarify the discontinuous record that the diaries provide. In doing so, I am aware that I, as editor, have assumed to some degree the responsibilities of authorship. And yet, the Dragon Master's instructions were, above all, to tell a story that would be of broad human interest, and I have attempted first and foremost to do this.

Difficulties arise also from the fact that some diary entries are in French, and, in the citation of some ancient texts, Chinese characters are used, or transliterated. I have thought it best to translate the French and to use modern English versions of the Master's brief citations from various classical Chinese texts. Specifically, these are: *Lao Tzu. Tao Te Ching*, trans. Gia-Fu Feng and Jane English (New York: Vintage, 1989); *The Book of Chuang Tzu*, trans. Martin Palmer with Elizabeth Breuilly (London: Penguin, 1996); *Lieh-Tzu*, trans. Eva Wong (Boston: Shambhala, 1995);

The Bodhidharma Anthology, trans. Jeffrey L. Broughton (Berkeley: University of California Press, 1999); *The Jade Emperor's Mind Seal Classic*, trans. Stuart Alve Olson (Vermont: Inner Traditions, 2003); *The Secret of the Golden Flower*, trans. Thomas Cleary (New York: Harper Collins, 1991); *The Diamond Sutra*, trans A. F. Price and Wong Mou-lam (Boston: Shambhala, 1999). Throughout, I have sought to establish a reasonable chronology, though dates are often missing from the source documents, or are incomplete. Consequently, I have sometimes made decisions based on what seems probable. For the most part, the handwriting is legible, but it can also be hasty and difficult to decipher, and abbreviations are frequently used. I have interpreted the unclear passages as best I can, and, throughout, for clarity, I have altered the abbreviations to Standard English.

The author of the diaries insisted on remaining anonymous. Consequently, I have used generic names (Father, Uncle, Sifu) or fanciful ones (Philippe, Krullo, Mei Lin). "We all have our stories," the Dragon Master says, and aren't all our stories, in the end, also always to some degree imagined?

WINTER GARDEN

I was his student. Shortly before he died in 2001, he gave me a collection of his papers – his diaries, he called them. They are made up of notebooks, sketch pads, binders, clipped-together collections of loose leaves, bundles of letters (sent and received), jumbled together in a large cardboard stationery box. Mostly, they are records of events in his life, brief essays, reflections, rough drafts of letters, quotations, desiderata. Everything is handwritten. Sometimes there are no dates, and sometimes only the month or the day.

"Use these to make a story," he said. "But not my story. Don't use my name. Make it a story about Kung-Fu. The real Kung-Fu." He gave me the box just as he was about to take a taxi to the airport. He knew that he was leaving London for Hong Kong for the last time. Within a month, I learned that he was dead.

At first, shortly after I received the box, I sorted through it to take stock, but I soon realised that I would need time to put such a great amount of material into order and to assess what kind of 'story' it might tell. Clearly, I would have to select, and supply missing links, either from my own recollections or by making enquiries. In short, the project would be demanding, and, initially, I was discouraged. Then, when I learned that the Dragon Master had died, my discouragement turned to grief and I felt as if, somehow, the desert had reclaimed an oasis by which I had been navigating for more than twenty years. And so, as a way of trying to regain some bearings, I returned to the box and began reading. Now, almost two years later, I begin the story, and, in order to do so, I have devised some simple strategies.

First, I place the documents, roughly, in chronological order, but if a late entry illuminates something that occurred earlier, I cite the late entry out of sequence. Second, where appropriate, I run excerpts together to make a continuous narrative. Third, I supply linking information, which, as much as possible, is based on facts that I know to be the case. When the facts are not clear, my conclusions are based on what seems probable, in light of the evidence.

As the Master requested, I do not use his name. Like every true follower of Shaolin Chan, he preferred anonymity. The ancient Chinese sage, Chuang Tzu says that 'the perfect man leaves no trace', and, in the same spirit, my instructions were not to write 'his' story, but, rather, a story about the way – the Tao – of Kung-Fu. Yet, paradoxically, the way can be followed only by the individuals who choose it, and the Master knew very well that I would not write a merely general account of the Art. Rather, I would write in such a manner that the Master's particular story would brighten into a broader, more typical significance. I will therefore begin by giving him a typical name.

He is Philippe Ming. On his mother's side he is Anglo and French Canadian, and on his father's, Chinese. He was born in 1920, in Montreal, and his mother was from a wealthy family. Her grandfather had made his fortune as a supplier for the trans-Canada railways in the mid and late 1800s. He had put together a lucrative business servicing the construction camps, thereby furthering the progress of the great iron horse across a vast continent. His success enabled him eventually to build a fine family home in Montreal, where his son, Philippe's grandfather, was born in 1857. Philippe's grandfather was also interested in commodities, but he went into finance, and towards the end of his career he travelled widely, sometimes as an official representative of Canada's business interests abroad.

Philippe's mother enjoyed a privileged and leisurely upbringing. She became an accomplished, though not exceptional, pianist, and she met Philippe's father after a chamber concert at the British Embassy in Ottawa. Because of her interest in music, she had been invited along by her parents. Her father had business to attend to during the following days, and, presumably, to ease the way towards the contentious meetings to come – which were mainly about war bonds – the first evening was a gala affair. And that was where the meeting took place between Philippe's mother and the man who was to become his father.

He was a career diplomat attached to the British Embassy. He was born in Guangzhou, in China, and his parents moved to Hong Kong when he was small. He was educated in a British school, and, from an early age, he spoke English. He also learned French, and, in his early twenties, he spent two years in Paris. His exceptional skills in Chinese, English, and French were a valuable asset in his diplomatic career, but, by nature he was reserved, withdrawn even. Nonetheless, his elegant appearance – tall and slender, with a slightly fastidious yet assured manner – instantly drew attention. When he was standing still, at repose, he appeared as if suspended, alert in the moment like some long-legged wading bird, its head warily raised, not readily approachable, yet captivating.

For Philippe's mother, the fascination of that first meeting at the embassy endured, and, two years later, the pair were married. In due course, in 1920, Philippe was born in Montreal, where he spent his early years. His father travelled, but had a more or less permanent base in Ottawa, and was able to stay – sometimes for a few weeks, sometimes a few days – with his new Montreal family. He was attentive, but, as was the case throughout his life, he seemed also always somehow at one remove, as if touched by some secret loneliness. But, for young Philippe, life was good. He attended a

Jesuit school, where his education was rigorous and humane. He was bilingual in French and English, and he learned elementary Chinese, which was to be the foundation for his immersion in that language during his teens, after he moved to Hong Kong.

The move to Hong Kong came about because Philippe's mother died. He was twelve years old at the time. An aneurism erupted in her brain and she was found sitting in an armchair, a piece of embroidery in her lap, the needle halfway through a stitch. She had been making a Chinese dragon for him, in green thread. For years, he kept it in a drawer, wanting to preserve it, and yet not to look at it.

Philippe's diaries begin in 1943, some three years after he returned to Montreal from Hong Kong, because of the war. But the only detailed recollection of his early childhood was written almost ten years after that, in the early 1950s, when, as we shall see, he experienced the most intense personal conflict of his adult life. The emotional turmoil caused by his childhood trauma returned then in force, and he writes about it in a diary entry from 1952.

DIARY MAY, 1952

I see myself again looking out the window of the Montreal house. The garden is a drift of greyish snow. The bare trees along the hedges gesture, crazily, like famished beggars. Inside the house it is warm, suffocating, but I know already that I have become that scene outside. My mother is dead, and I am cold, silent, angry. I remember the shock of my new discovery that there are evil things in the world from which your parents can't protect you. I remember also how Father retained his reserve, and how I found that both reassuring and infuriating. It was a source of strength that he was steady, but a sign of something wanting that he did not show emotion. I wanted him to feel something, and to teach me. But he glided about, wrapped up in himself as a tightly-rolled umbrella. Then he would whisper his Buddhist consolation: "Impermanence and sorrow, impermanence and sorrow."

At school, I was assigned meetings with Father Gilles, the spiritual director. By and large, my fellow students treated me as if I had an illness that might be contagious. Which is to say, they were sympathetic, but kept their distance. By contrast, Father Gilles asked me directly what I was feeling. I told him that I didn't understand why my mother had died. "It is impossible to understand God's ways," he said. "Suffering is a mystery – as great a mystery as the meaning of the universe itself. The truth is, to be alive is to suffer, and we don't know why this is so. But we also take comfort in the fact that Jesus suffered for us. His crucifixion tells us that he knows our pain and loss. He cried out that God – his own father – had abandoned him, and the meaning of his love for us would not be completely real unless his father did indeed abandon him. And so, in our suffering we take comfort in the knowledge that Jesus is with us, on our side. Think about his cross. Think about his resurrection."

'Impermanence and sorrow' – the Buddhist injunction. 'He died for us' – the Christian protest. At twelve years old I had no idea that these two sentences, spoken by these two fathers, would chart the course of much that would concern me afterwards.

But here, today, now again for me the whole world is in ruins, and I remember the two fathers only to be sure that once more they don't help, can't help with this other affliction in my life. Now I know for sure that love kills everything. She is the worst thing that has happened to me, and yet without her I am dying. The mysterious female is the gate of life, says Lao Tzu, and we have to return to her. But my mother died, and now I am dying also, of this insanity, this love, the deadliest force on earth.

We will return by and by to the events that caused Philippe such grief in the 1950s. For now, after his mother died, things did not go well for him in Montreal. He wasn't thriving at school. His father was often absent, and the inner stillness or self-containedness that seemed to make his father inaccessible mirrored, in another key, the son's angry silence. Philippe was well cared for, but the warmth of the Montreal house was no match for the wintery garden with which he had already identified his inner life.

And so, in 1934, he moved to Hong Kong, where he lived with his father's older brother, a well-to-do jade dealer. Philippe's uncle was unmarried. He lived, with two servants and a cook, in a fine, spacious house on Kowloon side. He was pleased to take his young nephew in, and it seems that from early on, Father and Uncle had hopes that Philippe by and by would enter the jade business.

In Hong Kong, Philippe attended a Jesuit school, which provided continuity with his education in Montreal. Uncle, however, was a Mahayana Buddhist, devoted especially to the bodhisattva Kwan Yin. He also believed that the perennial teachings of the world's great religions converged towards an ethic of non-selfishness and non-violence, and that we should treat others as we would like to be treated, while maintaining reverence for the mystery of life – the one source beyond words, dogmas, or creeds. Because of his broad outlook, Uncle was comfortable as the overseer of Philippe's Christian education, even though he knew that Philippe would also learn about other ways of thinking from the very fact that he was living in Uncle's house.

The 1943 diaries show that Uncle was correct about this. Philippe began writing his diaries while he was a student at McGill University, in Montreal, after he was evacuated from Hong Kong in late 1939. Like many Hong Kong residents, Uncle was aware that the Japanese invasion was imminent. By 1938, the Japanese navy was already sailing into Hong Kong territorial waters, and there had been attacks from the air on the Kowloon-Canton train. By mid-1940, the alarm was in full cry, and the government issued an evacuation order for women and children. But Uncle had acted early, and had time enough to put his entire jade collection into safe keeping, before closing his business and boarding up the premises. Philippe was sent back to Montreal, and Uncle made plans for a retreat to mainland China, which had its own dangers but was preferable to living under a Japanese occupation. He left the house in the care of a custodian, an old man who had made his living as a jade polisher and was a long-time acquaintance. With a small group of associates, Uncle then left for China, where he waited out the war.

For his part, Philippe had little understanding of why he was dispatched to Montreal in late 1939. He no doubt began his diaries a few years afterwards, in 1943, in order to help himself to come to grips with the upheaval not only in his own life, but also across the world, which had by then descended into all-out war. And so, in 1943, as he attempts to take stock, he describes his first sea voyage, in 1934, when he was fourteen, from Vancouver to Hong Kong. He does not name the ship, but it was probably one of the great 'White Empresses' of the Canadian Pacific Company that sailed from Vancouver to Hong Kong by way of Yokohama. His travelling companions were a retired Montreal banker and his wife, who were friends of Philippe's maternal family. They agreed to look after Philippe during the voyage and to see that he was safely delivered to his uncle in Hong Kong.

DIARY AUGUST-SEPTEMBER, 1943

I scarcely knew where Hong Kong was, or how far away. I did not imagine that endless ocean, that blue-grey horizon diffused into a blue-grey sky at some infinitely far distance, a pure emptiness. And yet I had to believe that somewhere beyond, in that emptiness, lay China. For now, the monotony of all that one could see in any direction so that direction itself became meaningless, the monotony of all that one could hear from the ceaseless, softly thudding engines – that monotony itself became strangely peaceful, consoling, and I found that I was, for the first time since I became unhappy, content. I was between places, free from commitment, hopes, fears. My guardians, the Pépins, were considerate, but they chose a strategy of benign neglect, which suited me well, and I think they knew that – which is perhaps why they chose it. There was a small library on board, and I read stories by Kipling and looked at maps of the Far East. I also enjoyed being alone on the upper deck, gazing at the vast expanse of nothingness all around, absorbed in the illusion of standing still, while behind me the three giant funnels stood like sentinels in service of the massive engines underneath, driving us forward like time itself; imperceptible, relentless.

The weather stayed fair, which was pleasing but also disappointing. There would be excitement in a squall or two. And yet I didn't want the reverie broken – the feeling of being suspended, neither here nor there.

***

Uncle's house is on Kowloon side. It was built by his father, a successful trader in tea and spices. At the time, Kowloon was not a desirable location. The more affluent residents of Hong Kong side by and large thought of it as a haven for smugglers, gangsters, and pedlars of assorted vice. But Uncle's father had seen the future, and he built himself a splendid stone mansion at an excellent price, in Hung Hom, overlooking Kowloon Bay, not far from Kowloon Station, which has rail links to Beijing, Shanghai, and Guangzhou. As with many buildings in Hong Kong, the style is eclectic. The red tile roof has something Mediterranean in it (a style probably borrowed from neighbouring Macao), though with a distinctive Chinese roofline. The façade is fronted by four neo-classical pillars which frame three small balconies on the upper storey, and, continuing to the ground floor, the pillars front a grand, recessed double door, with two tall windows on either side.

As the population of Kowloon soared and residential housing in Hung Hom became congested, a high stone wall, topped with a wrought iron railing, was built around the house, the value of which increased dramatically in the first few decades of the twentieth century. Behind the wall is a small garden, with a path of some sixty feet leading to four stone steps up to the front door, which is recessed between the pillars beneath a rounded arch carved with auspicious Chinese motifs. The garden path is hedged with low, carefully manicured ilex, and at the top of the steps are two large, glazed, plum-coloured urns with blazing white lion's mane chrysanthemums.

From the road, the façade is largely concealed by the wall, but when you enter through the gate, the building is immediately impressive, though not pretentious. Decades of gritty air, heavy with the dust from construction projects and moisture sucked up from the greasy bay by the overpowering heat has caused the exterior to look faded, smudged, distressed beyond its years. Yet the house stands quietly strong, all the more substantial and imposing the longer you look.

Inside, it is magical, and to this day I recall my introduction to that special enchantment. Throughout, it was fitted with antique furniture – old rosewood, mahogany, rattan – silk and brocade curtains, ornately inlaid screens, ceiling fans with vast wingspans, shining floors in merbau and teak, and a great collection of curiosities as well as statues of the buddhas and bodhisattvas, wall-hangings with illustrations of Lao Tzu, the Seven Sages of the Bamboo Grove, the Yellow Emperor and his helpers, dazzling calligraphic renditions of ancient Chinese poetry, assorted ceramics, rare carpets, a great variety of lamps, and, of course, choice pieces of jade. It was a collector's emporium, but Uncle did not treat it as if it were sacrosanct or untouchable, and his attitude to his possessions reflected the man himself. He was perpetually busy and curious, but he was also relaxed and accommodating. Before I met him, I imagined him on the model of Father. But he was quite different. He was not so tall but more compact, with a small but substantial round belly. He was restive and moved about constantly, his bright eyes assessing, crinkled at the corners as if he were perpetually on the edge of laughter, amused by whatever he was having to deal with at the moment. His hair was almost entirely grey, always unruly. At home, he preferred wearing a traditional Chinese gown, especially his favourite, made of plum-coloured silk with old-fashioned wide sleeves and cloth buttons, and sometimes it whistled softly as he swept by, in a hurry as usual. He was effortlessly talkative, and when we first met on the quay, after the boat docked, he greeted me as if I were completely familiar to him and as if my arrival were nothing out of the ordinary. His English was precise, though sometimes eccentric, and was accented in a manner I had not heard before. By contrast, my father had long since acquired an impeccable received pronunciation. But I was soon to encounter Uncle's manner of speaking in many other situations in Hong Kong.

Would I like tea now? Would I like to see the plants in the garden or visit the library? Did I play sports? There are many clubs in Hong Kong, and perhaps he could introduce me to some of them. He enquired about his brother, but didn't dwell on the topic. Instead, he wanted to know how I felt and what I thought. As we made our way through the rooms so that he could introduce me to the house, he paused now and then to tell me about some curiosity. Did I know much about jade? Look at that green dragon. Did I see how the lustre differed from the jade lamp beside it?

I didn't realise it at the time, but I now see that in this easy, amusing, friendly conversation, Uncle was hard at work finding out things about me that were not the sorts of things people declare directly. He was interested in tastes and prejudices, demeanour, curiosity, range of reference, as well as strategies for self-protection. But for me at the time, he appeared the soul of geniality and it was sufficient that I felt welcome and that I felt at home.

Philippe attended the Jesuit school, as planned, but the diaries do not have much to say about his experience there. They do, however, contain a few reflections on developments that Philippe found relevant to the self-assessment that caused him to begin writing his diaries in the first place. For instance, he seems to have done well enough at school, though he was not an especially committed student. In general, he found that the pupils were more diverse than in Montreal, but the Hong Kong Jesuits were also more doctrinaire, and religious instruction for Catholic students was more catechetical than philosophical, more concerned with dogma than with the life of the spirit. Perhaps some dimension of missionary self-consciousness – of being, as it were, in the Christian vanguard in a non-Christian Asia – had produced a leaner, more propositional version of the faith for teaching purposes than the more subtle, nuanced European teaching style that prevailed among the Jesuits in French Canada. If there was a Hong Kong version of Father Gilles, Philippe does not mention him, and although he would not forget what Father Gilles had told him, a different kind of claim was also beginning to be made, not by the Jesuit fathers, but by Uncle.

As far as I can tell, there were two main aspects to Uncle's plans for his nephew. The first (as I mentioned earlier) was to open the way for him eventually to enter the jade business. The second was to introduce him to the world of Kung-Fu – specifically, to the world of Shaolin Chan. And although Philippe's father remains a distant, perhaps enigmatic figure throughout our story, there is no doubt that he was in close communication with his brother, and that he knew more about Shaolin Chan than Philippe realised. Also, the brothers seem to have agreed that, for Philippe, change could best be brought about through continuity. The values of his Montreal education would not simply be jettisoned, not least because the special circumstances of Philippe's birth and upbringing offered the possibility of an enriched and enriching synthesis which should be developed responsibly, and not stunted or thwarted by the demands of a conveniently over-simplified allegiance either to East or West, Christian or Buddhist. Philippe's Kung-Fu – should he decide to take it up – would authenticate who he was as an individual person shaped by a particular history. However, in the years between 1934 and 1938 – that is, from the time of his arrival in Hong Kong until he left school and joined Uncle's business – Philippe was unaware of these further dimensions of the situation in which he was immersed. But, by 1943, as he looked back, he was already finding his way towards some more adequate understanding.

DIARY SEPTEMBER, 1943 – JANUARY, 1944

I wasn't much interested in school, but I did not want to embarrass Uncle or disappoint Father. In Montreal, I must have been in worse shape than I thought for Father to place his hopes in making so drastic a change. Still, he wasn't wrong. The newness and strangeness of Hong Kong certainly altered how I saw things – as if my inner kaleidoscope was given a twist so that the old facets fell into many new and unpredictable patterns. The seething, constant aggravation of the endless crowds, the suffocating heat, the unrelenting, hectic babble, the smells, the dense networks of entangling streets – all that was a challenge, exhilarating, intimidating.

Being half European and half Chinese also felt different in Hong Kong. In Montreal, I was an exotic, a flavour of the mysterious East. Also, the Christianity I was taught there was complex, intricate, secure in its European roots. In Hong Kong, paradoxically, I sometimes felt more self-conscious about being Chinese, probably because I discovered that my Cantonese was not good enough and I felt I was, somehow, not true to myself if I couldn't speak it well. At school, religious instruction was narrower and simpler. I learned for the first time about Jesuit martyrs in China, and I was encouraged to pray for martyrdom – instant sainthood, worth the pains. Yet, during those years my eyes were opening to other, different ways of seeing. To my surprise, my European side was regarded for the most part as a worldly advantage – an opening to better business opportunities, for instance; a silver spoon, not a mystery.

At the time, I didn't think much about these things, but when I did, I could feel the cross-currents, the tensions by which I now know every human person is made up. Without yet quite belonging, I felt, somehow, that I was in the right place.

***

Uncle was busy and I didn't see him a lot. At home, the servants took care of the day-to-day routines. I had friends at school, and I do not remember feeling isolated or lonely. I knew that Uncle was absorbed in his work. He was always eager to explain the intricacies of a deal, the peculiarities of government regulations, how to describe the provenance and quality of some new piece he had acquired. Without realising it, I was getting a feel for his world, and not just in a business sense but through his conversations about the significance and the history of jade itself. I learned about its varieties, about grinding, cutting, polishing, its ritual uses and how it links us humans to the heavens, about dragon-tigers, flying horses and apsaras, and a host of mythological and symbolic motifs and details. "Here," Uncle said, taking me by the arm as we walked into his library, where he carefully lifted a magnificent carving from one of the shelves. "Look at that marvellous dragon. The woman standing on it. She is KwanYin, a revered bodhisattva; do you know what that is? No? Well, a bodhisattva is a person who has attained enlightenment and has escaped the perpetual cycle of life and death in our suffering world. Yet a bodhisattva chooses to be reborn and to return to the world, and will continue to do so until all the suffering in our world and every other world is healed."

I remember thinking, *That is a tall order for those bodhisattvas* and, then, also *What a noble and touching idea*. I asked for her name again, and what she was doing on the dragon.

"Her name is Kwan Yin. She is the bodhisattva of compassion. In her right hand she has a branch of willow to show how flexible she is, and her tears for the world are also those of the weeping willow. In her left hand she has a little vase. It is full of healing liquor, the nectar of compassion that she pours on us suffering creatures. Here, she stands on a dragon but she is not always depicted that way. In this case, she is calming the turmoil, the fierce energy at the source of creation. Yes, the world is a nightmare of suffering, but see how she stands tall, how the drapery flows, reflecting the shape – and also the meaning – of the willow."

"It is a lovely idea."

"Not just an idea. A fact. Try it and see." He was laughing, perhaps with a touch of amused self-mockery, as he placed the statue back on the shelf.

Afterwards, I began to notice that there were representations of Kwan Yin throughout the house, and as I got to know more, I came to see how, in her many varieties, she was in fact all around us – as Uncle said. Also, as I thought about the statue in the library, I found myself thinking about Father Gilles. He too had talked about compassion. Christ's cross and Kwan Yin belong, somehow, together, and I felt this more – how can I say it – in my imagination, as a sort of dawning awareness, rather than as something I could explain.

***

If Uncle had designs, he did not declare them. He was a good governor in the way Lao Tzu prescribes, because he seemed not to govern at all. I do believe, however, that I was in fact choosing in conformity with a plan that I didn't recognise, and which was of his making. Also, in the further background, I am sure that Father was every bit as aware of that plan as Uncle was.

Meanwhile, the school had fulfilled its function. By the time I left I was passably literate, numerate, and with a coherent if limited store of information about general subjects as well as the principal doctrinal claims, with their underpinnings in philosophical theology, of the One Holy Catholic and Apostolic Church. As both Father and Uncle explained, the Jesuits in Hong Kong continued the work of the Jesuits in Montreal. Yet not only the school curriculum and teaching remained familiar – so did my Montreal inner landscape, the grey-white snowdrift in the garden with the black trees that I preferred to the comforts of the domestic interior. In Hong Kong I still sought the protection of that chilly refuge. I am sure Uncle also knew this – again, like Lao Tzu's wise ruler, who knows his people better than they know themselves.

Although we did not spend a great deal of time together, my path crossed with Uncle's quite often, especially in the evenings. As ever, he was engaging, interested in what I had to say, questioning, quietly merry, with the twinkling humour that made him seem friendly and accessible even as he also danced just out of reach. I continued to learn about jade, and he continued to cultivate my interest. The wonderful house with its vast collection of antiques and curiosities went on providing no end of opportunities for conversations about history, mythology, religion, art. There were carved buddhas from Thailand and Cambodia, stupas from Ceylon that told the story of the intricate interplay of Hinduism, Buddhism and colonialism, ivories from Mogul India, bewildering Tibetan mandalas with endlessly fertile genealogies of gods and demons, mysterious Chinese Taoist alchemical diagrams, bodhisattvas from the Mahayana traditions, Japanese swords and Shaolin staffs, dorjes and bells, incense burners, altars – including a grand butsudan decorated with carved stone and bronze – brilliant tapestries of the Pure Land. Our conversation developed naturally and easily around these and countless other topics, interconnected through a vast web of ever-expanding, endlessly fascinating associations and patterns.

During one of these conversations, Uncle paused before a table in the hallway, where, among an assortment of smaller ornaments stood a wooden statue of a fierce-looking old man, striding, with a staff over his shoulder. A bundle was tied to the end of his staff, indicating, I presumed, that he was itinerant. His head was bald, but he had a shaggy beard and wild, glaring eyes, which the carver had exaggerated.

"Look at him!" Uncle pointed, mimicking the confrontational energy of the man himself. "What would you do if you met that one?"

"Stand aside," I said.

"He has two names. In India, he is Bodhidharma, and in China, Ta Mo. I think of him as Ta Mo, but there is no need to choose. He lived in the sixth century, as far as anyone knows, but we can't be sure. He brought a certain style of Buddhism – called Chan – to China, and introduced it to the famous Shaolin Temple, that has existed to the present. But it has been destroyed recently and the monks have had to flee. Many were killed. It is a tragedy. Still, as you see, Ta Mo is fierce, and the spirit of resistance is in him. Wherever he went he was a non-conformist and he kept giving offence and getting turned out of the house. His style of Buddhism puts a lot of emphasis on meditation, but he also brought some physical exercises from India, and he taught these to the monks to help to keep them healthy. He thought that in order to meditate well, it is a good thing to stay well physically. Or as well as possible. But he thought of the physical exercises also as an aid to meditation – indeed, that is their main point. Ta Mo is also said to have retreated to a cave for nine years to stare at a wall. It is not clear what this 'wall-watching' means, but obviously it has to do with meditation. Perhaps it is a metaphor for attention without distraction. Some stories even say that Ta Mo cut off his eyelids so that he could stare at the wall without blinking. But that can't be true, and it certainly must be a metaphor along the same lines as wall-watching. Still, you often see Ta Mo, as here, with bulging eyes. Personally, I think they show his determination. You have to be determined if you are going to go seriously into meditation."

"Do you meditate, Uncle?"

"Yes. Not enough. I have a room behind the bedroom."

"What exercises did Ta Mo bring? Do monks still use them?"

"Nobody knows what the original exercises were. Some think they must have been based on yoga and that there was an emphasis on breathing. Others imagine a mixture of stretching and calisthenics to get the body moving and the blood circulating. It's all a guess, because the temple was destroyed in the seventeenth century, and the old practices cannot be recovered with any degree of certainty. Also, the original exercise routines themselves developed and changed over the years. As to the second part of your question: yes, the monks have kept exercising right down to the present day. Sometimes, the exercises are called Kung-Fu. But that can be misleading, because the tradition has so many fake imitators. Charlatans and bullies have taken over bits and pieces of it, and they put it up for sale on street corners and call it Kung-Fu. In fact, they know even less about Kung-Fu than they did before they began to practise the stupid things they do in its name."

I had heard the term 'Kung-Fu' at school, in connection with boxing, and I had taken it as a name for different kinds of Asian fighting methods. But it meant nothing to me beyond the chatter of schoolboys. And so I was surprised by what Uncle was telling me about this gruff old fellow carved out of wood on the hall table. I was even more surprised when, in the act of turning away to continue down the hall, he remarked: "The real thing is very beneficial. Perhaps you might try it?" He had said the same thing about Kwan Yin. This time, I replied.

"How might I do that?"

"I must run," he said, "But later, if you still want to know how, ask me again."

***

I was curious about Kung-Fu because I was surprised that Uncle was interested in it, and also because I knew so little about it. What kind of society had that old itinerant founded in the sixth century? And what was his carved image doing among the Buddhas and Bodhisattvas and the other mythological figures throughout the house? And so, the day after our conversation about Ta Mo, I brought up the subject again.

"I have been thinking. Ta Mo was a monk and he meditated and did exercises. But isn't Kung-Fu about fighting?"

"There are different ways of fighting. Sometimes you have to fight against yourself, for instance."

"But Kung-Fu is real fighting. Punches, kicks. No? The boys at school talk about people who know Kung-Fu, and how they fight in the street. Some of the boys say they know it, or parts of it."

"Well, the first thing about Kung-Fu is that you don't go around chattering about it. This conversation, for instance, is not something that you would discuss with those boys. Besides, those boys don't know what they are talking about, and the fact that they chatter like that shows that they don't know."

"For sure, they don't talk about anything like that statue, or Ta Mo's society, whatever it is. But I realise that I don't know anything and I would like to know more."

"Think longer. Tell me in one month – not a day before – where your thoughts take you. Also, tell me how you imagine what kind of society Ta Mo founded. This is not an assignment. It is not school. Meanwhile, let us not talk more about it, so that you can think – or not, as you choose."

Uncle's usual friendliness had now taken on an undertone that was almost stern; off-putting, even. I had long understood that, as a hard-headed businessman, he was capable of being tough, and I had seen signs of that. Still, it was unlike him to set out conditions as brusquely as he had just done, and I felt that the invitation was not inviting at all. And so I decided then and there to let the whole thing go.

As I was soon to discover, however, sometimes deciding to let things go causes them to stick around all the more persistently. 'Don't think of an elephant' is a good way of ensuring that you won't get the image of an elephant out of your mind anytime soon. In short, I found myself continuing to think about Ta Mo, how our enemies can be within ourselves, why people are violent and how there seems to be no end to the pain we inflict on one another. The suffering Jesus and the compassionate Kwan Yin became part of a confused, inner conversation. But there was a further conversation as well, having to do with actual, physical combat. Never mind the statues and ideas – how satisfying it would be to disable someone who threatened you, to disarm or smash your enemies into submission with techniques that loudmouths claim to know but don't, and that can be taught to chosen insiders. As the days went by, violent fantasies were increasingly confused in my mind with the questions I had raised and was supposed to answer. Then, eventually, of its own accord, the whole train of thought slowed down, and after a couple of weeks, it had dwindled almost entirely away.

***

It was almost a month since Uncle asked me to choose whether or not to continue our conversation. For the second half of the month, I hadn't given much consideration to Ta Mo or Kung-Fu. Still, I thought that perhaps it would be best, out of courtesy, to raise the topic again with Uncle if only to lay it aside as something that I wasn't going to pursue.

Shortly before dinner, I found him in the library. It held a collection of several thousand books, most of which were specialised, and he often spent time there, working on business plans, drafting memoranda, or reading. I hesitated to interrupt him, but it was one month to the day, and if he meant what he said, he would remember that. As agreed, he would expect me to take the initiative.

"It is one month," I said. He looked up with a small gesture of feigned surprise, and the same light, ironising chuckle.

"So it is. I had forgotten. Come in. Take a chair. Now, what do you think?"

I decided to be plain. "At first, I thought quite a lot. But there is too much that I don't know. I thought about Ta Mo and Kwan Yin, and about why people fight. I didn't decide anything. Then I thought I might want to be a fighter, to defeat my enemies, to be strong. After a while, I stopped thinking about that too. Almost. I didn't talk to anyone. I have no idea what you meant when you said, 'Try it'. In fact, I came to tell you that I was thinking about not trying it. But now I have to say, well, at least, I would like to know more."

He listened, his familiar, animated gestures stilled for a moment as he took in what I said. Then, simply, almost casually, he replied.

"We can arrange something." A further pause, as he took stock. "I will introduce you to a teacher. He is young. I think you will like him. You will need to set aside one hour, three days a week to meet with him. And then half an hour on the other days to practise what he shows you. After six weeks, we will see if you want to go on. If not, as I said before, that is OK. Also, you can discontinue at any time during the six weeks. If you do discontinue, it will be over. No questions asked. But no going back."

He stopped, raising his eyebrows in a quizzical gesture. I was discomposed by the swiftness with which things had moved, confused by the sheer clarity and directness of the proposal. Then I added to my own confusion by the answer I gave.

"All right," I said. "I'll try."

"It's an adventure, Philippe, and after today, it's out of my hands. But I can give you a pointer or two before you get going. As you now understand, it is important that you yourself make the choice. You will keep having to choose, until you might one day discover that you have been chosen as well, and then conscious choice goes out of the picture. What you are undertaking requires a lot of practice, and you will meet obstacles. You have already met the first, which, as you see, I put in your way myself. Remember, you can discontinue at any time. Think of it as trying some new kind of food. If it is not to your taste, nobody will be interested in making you eat it, and nobody who knows you will serve it to you again. Finally, as I said, we do not talk about Kung-Fu to outsiders. Once I introduce you to your teacher, all will be between you and him and I will be an outsider then. I will have no direct interest in what you are doing, and whether you go on or stop will be a matter of indifference to me. Our lives in the house, and your life at school, will be as usual. All this might seem a little strange, but in the long run it will make sense. Now, talking of food, it is almost time for dinner. I must say before we go that I am pleased that you came today, and I wish you luck."

***

That morning, I walked with Uncle through the alleyways of Mung Kok. I was to take my bearings from Kowloon Station, not far from the house, because the station was a landmark that I could easily find. Then we went north, away from the pandemonium of rickshaws, taxis, porters, railway traffic and travellers, into the tangle of streets with which Uncle seemed completely familiar. He paused to point out key markers along the way, and he had jotted these down on a sheet of paper, for my future reference. At the best of times, the heat of Hong Kong was oppressive, but here it was truly unbearable – a sweltering stew of garbage, cooking smells, vegetable stalls, exhaust fumes; dust-laden, suffocating air trapped in the claustrophobia of the packed buildings. Added to that was the confusion of the seething crowds, the clamour of businesses pushing their wares out into the street – tailors, electronics repair shops, hawkers of clocks and watches, haberdashers, vendors of dried fish and duck meat, roasted chickens, candied fruits, emporiums crammed with knick-knacks, furniture stores, doorways and awnings hung with banners and streamers, and everywhere also fugitive hints, a sinister atmosphere of the hidden dealings of Triads and snakeheads, of smuggled goods and available, forbidden pleasures and addictions. It all seemed a world away from the quiet rooms and the big ceiling fans of the house. And yet we had walked for less than twenty minutes.

"The way seems crooked," Uncle said, "but actually it's not. On your journey back, it will always be slightly downhill from here. So, if you are not sure, or if you miss a landmark, go back roughly in the downhill direction – the small streets won't matter. The gradual slope will take you to Kowloon Station, or close by. Then you'll have your bearings, and you'll be home. Now we just need to go through here." He pointed to an alleyway, at the end of which was a storage building that looked like a garage. The door was dull red, gleaming against the seasoned and cracked wooden exterior, and the building was separated from the alley by a high iron fence, with a gate. "Here," said Uncle, as he went in ahead of me. He ventured no further than the doormat on the other side of the entrance. Almost immediately, from another door at the back of the building, a young Chinese man appeared. He was in his early twenties, about five feet seven inches tall. He looked fit, and he moved with an unselfconscious, soft athleticism that I came by and by to recognise was shared by many Kung-Fu practitioners. He wore a black cotton uniform, with loose pants and a top cinched with a red sash.

"This is Leung, your teacher," Uncle said, with a slight bow to the young man. "Leung, this is Philippe, and I hand him over to you. He knows his way back, and the hours that we agreed for you both to meet." With that, Uncle bowed again. And when Leung returned the bow, Uncle left.

"Good day. It is pleasant to make your acquaintance."

Leung's English was good, more heavily accented than Uncle's, but he was less than entirely fluent, so that his attention to correctness could make him sound a little stilted. He seemed to pick up on what I was thinking.

"For our sessions we will do in English. Maybe some Chinese. Afterwards, in the higher class, just Chinese, if for you it is possible, of course." He smiled with a kind of happy buoyancy. "First, you know, we take our shoes off and set them there, on the mat. Then, always, when we come in we bow to the place inside, like this." He stood beside me, and with his left hand cupped and closed over his right fist, with both hands held before him at chest level, he bowed briefly, facing into the practice hall. "Like this," he said.

And so we began. I learned the bow – which, I was told, should be repeated on leaving – and also the routine with the shoes. The interior of the hall (I'll call it that) did indeed resemble a garage, but the floor was polished wood, excellently maintained. Some of the walls had cupboards, and there was a set of bookshelves at the back, on the left. On the right was a full-length mirror, and a narrow door between the mirror and the bookshelves led to a tiny kitchen with utensils for making tea. There were also tins of dry goods – biscuits, candied fruit. Some cupboards in the hall had cleaning equipment: buckets, brushes, cloths, polish, soap. In an open space between the cupboards on the right-hand side there were racks with weapons – staffs of different sizes, and swords.

"Every day we sweep a little," Leung said. "Now and then we

scrub and polish. So everything is spick and span. Tea and water as we like. Here." He handed me a brush. "We sweep here to here, then here to here. This pan is for what you sweep. It goes to the bin behind the kitchen. You get going, and I get tea going." He smiled, pleased at his little wordplay.

It was a small space, and sweeping it didn't take long. There was vitually nothing to pick up in the dustpan, but I went through the motions. I then put the brush and pan back into the cupboard. In the kitchen, there was just enough room for two small folding chairs, and we used the counter top as a table for the teacups. Leung talked eagerly, but not on the topics I expected. He wanted to know about cricket, which he had seen played on Hong Kong side, and had read about. He liked sailing and talked about that too, though he used terms for Chinese boats that I didn't understand. He wanted to know about travelling across the Pacific on a liner, and about Canada. I soon felt that I was a source of information, an exotic visitor from whom he was eager for news. Then, after we had drunk several cups of tea and talked about many things but not about Kung-Fu, all at once he announced that today's lesson was over. I thought at first that he was making another little joke, alluding to the fact that I had been instructing him rather than the reverse. But he wasn't. "Time to go." He stood up, and as a prelude to bidding me farewell, he added "Loose pants, please. Loose shirt, same as now. No uniform required. And don't forget, please to bow out."

He stood at the kitchen door as I crossed the floor to get my shoes. I guessed I had better bow before I put them on, though I wasn't sure. So that is what I did. The first lesson was over.

**

As Uncle indicated in advance, he did not enquire about how things went with Leung, though there was a general, polite acknowledgement that the lessons were, in fact, under way. Did I manage to make it home without difficulty? How much time did I think I should allow to get there? Would I like to take some fruit next time? Or an umbrella? I answered matter of factly, signalling back to him that I understood that he did not want to get into the details of what actually went on.

The next lesson began with another sweep of the floor that didn't need sweeping. Leung then positioned me in front of him, in the middle of the hall. He showed me what he called the attention stance – feet shoulder width apart, hands lightly clasped behind the back. When instructions are being given, a student is to stand like this. A neutral stance is when the hands are unclasped and held at the sides with the feet closer together.

In the role of instructor, Leung's manner changed. His tone and attitude made him appear somehow older, more capable. During that first conversation, when he was going on about cricket and sailboats, I felt that we were equals. Now we weren't.

"We begin with the bow," he said, and we bowed to each other. "Welcome to Kung-Fu. You know the meaning, 'Kung-Fu'?"

I knew that in themselves the words didn't mean a lot. 'Hard work', or 'skill', is a loose translation. I opted for the simple answer: "Hard work. Mainly."

"Yes," he said. "Also, doing a thing well. Doing a thing with skill that comes from practice. All kinds of things can be Kung-Fu. Doing a task properly, handling a problem with a good result. That also is 'good Kung-Fu'. Here, we don't use the word much. We call it the Art. But as you please. The definition doesn't matter. Practice matters." He paused, and then went on.

"First, the horse stance. I show you. Then tell you."

He stepped into a deep horse stance. I saw straight away in his alignment and poise as he held the stance, how powerful his legs were, and how lightly his upper body appeared to rest on – even as it was also charged by – the strength that underpinned it. He held the stance for ten seconds or so, and then returned to neutral.

"So. From neutral stance. Chamber your hands at your hips,

fists closed, backs of hands facing down. Like this. Now, imagine a barrel at your left side. You have to step over it with your left leg. Like this – high, and step to the left. Step as far as comfortable."

He took the step, his knee springing high, effortlessly, as his leg swept in an arc to the left and his feet settled into the stance, much wider apart than his shoulders.

"From here, sit as far as you can. Comfortably. Back straight. Think of a line, a string, running from the top of your head, down through your spine into the floor. That is your centre line. Think of your stance and the centre line together, so that the stance is shaped around the centre line. Whatever trouble you have with the stance, remember, the centre line comes first. Now… together."

I followed him into the stance, but I couldn't step as wide as I wanted and I couldn't sit deeply at all. Keeping my back straight was going to be a problem. After a few seconds, we returned to neutral.

"Again," he said. "This time, watch also your feet. Your feet need to point straight ahead. So: on the count, take the stance, then fix your feet."

We took the stance. Again, I felt the same pressures and awkwardness, and when I attended to my feet, I saw that they were pointing slightly outwards. I needed to make them parallel, and this proved impossible to do without closing the stance a little. As I made the adjustment, I felt the outsides of my lower legs taking the pressure.

"Neutral," he said. I stood back up, hands by my sides. "The points to remember. Step left over the barrel. Feet wider than shoulders, as far as you can, comfortably. Feet pointing forward, parallel. Sit, back straight, hands chambered. Centre line holds everything together. Breathe naturally. That is all there is. Easy."

I had no idea of just how un-easy it was going to be.

We practiced taking the stance and holding it for about twenty seconds. Each time, Leung checked the details, calling my attention to points that needed adjustment until I began to get the feel of it, so that my mind did the checking, quite rapidly scanning then making the necessary alterations. Strangely, given that I was hardly moving, after a while I was out of breath, and my legs were trembling even when I stood up and relaxed.

"Good," said Leung. "Now sweep. We want the floor to smile, yes?" I wasn't sure I wanted the floor to smile, but I was glad enough to do the sweeping. After five minutes or so, Leung called out, "Again. Practise," and I understood that the point was less the smiling floor than getting my legs moving, while providing a task for me to focus on, before we went back to the stance.

Leung now asked me to hold the stance for as long as I could. I'm not sure how long I lasted – perhaps a minute – before my legs started to burn and shake. My back and rear-end were clenched and uncomfortable, and I had to struggle to keep my feet straight and my centre balanced.

"Break! And, neutral." I stood up. "Relax." We waited a minute, and then did it again. And again. Now I was sweating quite a bit, and really feeling the strain. But just when I felt that I definitely could not manage another repetition, Leung again rang the changes. "Sweep," he said. "Smiling floor."

I swept the floor, I have to say, with something close to gratitude. But then, back to the stance. The details. The burning that turned into a red-hot inner scream, until Leung again sensed the limit, sending me once more plodding up and down with the brush. I remember having a quietly desperate feeling that this was never going to end. But then it did.

"Time to go. Practise at home. Hold, make corrections, repeat. Half hour is enough, off and on, as you can."

On the walk home, I was feeling very little enthusiasm for Kung-Fu. I recalled how Uncle had assured me that I could quit, no questions asked. Now I was asking myself plenty of questions. And not just on that day, but in the long weeks that followed.

***

Writing things down brings back not just the memory, but also some of the feelings that were part of what happened. I had forgotten how difficult the emotional side of those six weeks was. Sometimes I felt so disheartened that I was certain that I must quit. The only thing we did, and the only thing I practised at home for the entire period was that same, boring, excruciating stance. When my legs burned out, I swept the floor, and when I had done that, it was back again to burning out the legs. Leung kept an eye on all the same details – fix this, change that, further here, straighter there, out here, in there. After the first couple of weeks, I felt only revulsion from the whole, tedious rigmarole, and the only thing that kept me going was the expectation that we would soon, surely, move on to something different. But in fact, there was to be nothing different. Moreover, Leung didn't explain anything. I didn't want to complain, but after yet another round of the smiling floor, and when I simply dreaded getting back into the stance, I told him: "I'm not sure I can take a lot more of this. Honestly." I tried to sound agreeable, even a little pathetic.

His reply was cheerful but dismissive: "Up to you." He paused, to let that sink in. "Now, practise. Don't worry about anything else." And so I realised that I would simply have to make up my mind to be in or out. And Leung was not going to help me with that.

As the days passed, it was small consolation to realise that I was improving. I held the stance for longer, and I felt it becoming deeper and wider. Still, over and over, the same limits kept being tested, the same adjustments being made. As a coping strategy, I decided to put out of my mind any further thoughts whatsoever about anything different, including the number of days left in the six weeks, the number of minutes left in the practice period. All that mattered was the task – the stance, the adjustments, the walking up and down with the brush – and putting out of my mind all the reasons why I should bid Leung goodbye.

By contrast, now, as I write this, I am nostalgic about Leung.

The fact is that the deep horse stance is the indispensable foundation – the strength, stability, groundedness that are built in because of it are the base of a pyramid, and everything else rests on that base. Also, there is another kind of foundation that gets set down in addition to the mechanics of the stance itself. Mental endurance – for want of a better way of putting it – is also a foundation. During those weeks, I struggled with my feelings as much as with the physical challenge, until, eventually, I found that centring and deepening the physical stance gave me the information I needed to centre and stabilise my feelings and my mind. Still, even now, I don't understand why I did in fact stay. All I know for sure is when I thought most seriously about quitting, I also felt angry. Angry about things I couldn't describe. What does it mean to say that anger got me through?

HONG KONG HOUSES

The diaries do not provide further information about the initial phase of Philippe's training, or how he took his leave of Leung. The exact dates are not clear, but we know that he was seventeen when he began training at the 'garage', and, the following year, he left school and entered Uncle's business as a full-time apprentice. After the war, he would travel extensively on Uncle's behalf. But in 1938-39, while he was still learning about the jade business in Hong Kong, his practice of the Art entered a new phase, which almost certainly began shortly after his initial six-week trial. Once again, Philippe was asked to choose before committing himself, and, as before, Uncle was the mediator. There was to be a new training venue, and a different teacher – or teachers. Although Philippe would meet Leung again, he would not do so as Leung's student.

In general, the period between 1938 and 39 was a happy time for Philippe. He was deeply involved in his Kung-Fu practice, and he was captivated also by what he was learning about Uncle's business. Those two worlds – Kung-Fu and jade – would remain interwoven throughout his career. Here, now, in his own words, is what he writes about the new developments.

DIARY MARCH-MAY, 1944

Uncle kept my training at arm's length, but he also wanted me to know that he had an eye on things. And so, when the six-week session with Leung was over, Uncle asked how I liked it. I said that 'like' wasn't the first word that came to mind, but I could see the benefits – though I was puzzled by a number of things.

"Ah, with puzzles the main thing is, do you want to work them out? Now you have finished with Leung. Perhaps you might try another puzzle?"

I didn't much fancy anything resembling those six weeks, and I thought I should say so.

"I'm not sure I could go through that again."

"The intensity of the first time is never repeated," Uncle said. "Look around you. Without foundations, this house would not have stood. And then it could not be a home for the art you see here. Foundations are set only once. Then the art has a home." The familiar tone of amusement flickered through his words, gently taunting. But, then, all at once he was on the move again.

"A dealer from Beijing. It's getting to be hard because of the war." As he turned away, hurrying off to his appointment, he tossed me a parting remark, over his shoulder, in the same fashion as before. "I will arrange a meeting at the end of the week. Let me know if you would rather not."

I saw that the game had changed, however slightly: now I was being invited to choose to prevent the arrangement from going ahead, rather than to agree to it being made in the first place. And, yes, I rather liked the idea of another puzzle.

***

Uncle introduced me to Sifu in one of the living rooms in the house. We sat on antique rosewood chairs, with a small table between us, on which tea was served. Sifu seemed old, but I couldn't be sure of his age – over sixty-five, certainly. He had a small, wispy grey beard and sparse grey hair. He was tall, with delicate hands and long fingers. The physical contrast with Uncle was striking – the long, slender man standing at ease, almost still, and the short, compact man restlessly mobile, as ever. They could have been a comic duo, a music-hall act. Sifu talked mostly in Chinese, though he made some concessions, for my benefit, in English. In return, I used Chinese, though I sometimes struggled to keep up, as he shifted between Cantonese and his native Mandarin. Both Sifu and Uncle were dressed in traditional clothes. When Uncle was at home, he preferred traditional dress, though at work he always wore the best quality Western business suits. Today, I wasn't sure if he was being casual, or if this was a different kind of business meeting.

Sifu talked about my school, my interest in jade, and the visit Father was due to make to Hong Kong in the coming weeks. He talked about Montreal, the unrest in Europe, rising prices in the local markets, and whether the coming summer would be more humid than the last. It seemed that he wanted to discuss anything except what I took to be the reason for our meeting. I went along politely, and Uncle and Sifu did most of the talking because, by and large, they knew more about the topics under discussion than I did. Perhaps an hour went by, and I realised that we probably weren't going to talk about Kung-Fu at all. Yet, one small, accidental event sticks in my mind almost as vividly today as when it happened.

The servant who brought the tea had come to collect the dishes. We had each eaten a macaroon from the plate on which they were served, and several were left over. When the servant lifted the plate, it tipped, and one of the macaroons skidded off and fell, close to Sifu's chair. I didn't see it happen, except for a flick of his sleeve. But when Sifu raised his hand, the macaroon sat gently between his thumb and index finger. He had plucked it out of the air between the plate and the floor without seeming to move at all. He had remained almost entirely still – except for the flick of the wide sleeve – and he placed the macaroon on the servant's tray, with a slight nod to the man, but without interrupting the conversation, which went on as if nothing had happened.

By and by, Sifu announced that it was time to go, and rose to leave. It had been a great pleasure, he said. Did I know that he had an old house, not unlike this one though not so interesting. From here, it would be perhaps a half-hour walk, or slightly less. And so, he was gone.

After he had seen Sifu out, Uncle went to the library, and came back with a sheet of paper on which was drawn a sketch of the streets between our house and Sifu's.

"You begin at this address, on Monday. You attend classes four days a week. Two more days you practise there, by yourself. And one day is free. Again, dear Philippe, you don't have to say yes. It is up to you. If you do not arrive at the class, Sifu will take that as 'No', and so will I. It will not be a problem, and you will hear no more about it."

***

And so I began. The route to Sifu's house was not difficult, and with the map to assist me, I found my way easily. The house was similar to Uncle's but bigger, and less impressive both in its architecture and in the interior. It was a simple, rectangular wood and brick structure, with a tiled roof and a plain façade with rows of identical windows. Stone steps led to the front door, and, as with Uncle's house, the building was separated from the road by a wall. The narrow space between the wall and the house was paved, and there were some decorative urns, but the general effect was austere. The inside was roomy and carefully maintained. Throughout, the wood floors shone with a rich, polished lustre. *Smiling*, I thought. Leung would be pleased. Mainly, the ground floor consisted of a large open area that served as the training hall. The interior architecture had been altered so that the space could be opened up by removing a wall and redistributing the load to a newly-installed post and beam structure. Behind the training hall were change rooms and a kitchen. The rest of the house consisted of various rooms and hallways, stairs and landings. Everything was sedately but tastefully decorated and appointed. The smell of polish carried a slight undertow of something astringent, perhaps carbolic, and from some recess on the upstairs floor, a faint scent of sandalwood incense drifted down.

When I arrived, I was admitted by a servant. Several other boys of roughly my age or a few years older were already present. I was introduced to one of them, a Eurasian like myself, called Rick. He seemed to be in his early twenties. He introduced me to the others, and then showed me the change rooms. I was invited to choose a uniform from shelves labelled 'small', 'medium', 'large'. Rick explained that the uniform now belonged to me. It would shrink at first, in the wash, which is why I should choose a size that initially felt too large. I learned how to wrap the white belt twice round my waist, and how to tie it in front. Then we rehearsed the bow and the attention stance. Rick said that there were thirteen students in the class, which would start in half an hour. My appointment had been arranged so that I would arrive early in order to learn the procedures.

I learned that there were three groups, each of thirteen students. Sometimes one or two students might move from one group to another, but the groups themselves did not interact. Everyone was to make progress at his own pace, according to ability and aptitude. The colour of a belt indicated the amount of knowledge acquired by a student, so that during skill sessions, when students worked in pairs, it would be clear who was in charge. In Kung-Fu the more advanced student always attempts to raise the level of the less advanced one. This means that a stronger student will never try to overwhelm a weaker one, but, instead, will work just above the level of the less experienced one, in order to be encouraging and, at the same time, challenging. Competitiveness has nothing whatsoever to do with making progress in the Art. Gradually, the traditional forms or *kuen*, will be introduced, and, as training progresses, each student will eventually make a certain *kuen* his own as an expression of his particular abilities.

The instructor of our group is called Kai, and I would meet him just before the beginning of class. In the coming weeks, however, Rick was to teach me, personally, in a separate room dedicated to one-on-one instruction. I would join the class for the opening warm-up exercises – rotations, bending, arm-swinging, and so on. Then Rick would teach me the basic techniques – the core vocabulary, as it were – on which the system is built. During class, these techniques are practised over and over by the group as a whole. Through repetition, the basics become as deeply built-in as the words we learn as children and to which we don't attend directly when we converse at a later stage. During the second part of the class, various techniques are combined, under Kai's instruction, into different units or 'skills'. Students work in pairs to learn and practise these skills, which eventually are reconfigured into forms, or *kuen*. The forms are choreographed routines, and a certain level of skill is necessary before a *kuen* is taught. The forms themselves have different levels of difficulty, corresponding, roughly, to the belt levels. Rick insisted that the *kuen* are of great importance, and must be learned patiently, and then endlessly repeated. They are checked and corrected frequently by the instructors. Each move needs to be exact, and the movement of the whole must be learned as if it were a dance. After many repetitions, a student will perform the movements without thinking about them, and, then, after many more repetitions – perhaps over a period of years – the form will adapt itself to the student, just as the student adapted to it at the beginning. "There is much more to learn about all this,"

Rick said, "and there is a great deal that I can't tell you, because I myself don't know." Finally, on the two days of each week when I would not be attending class, the hall would be available for free practice. I was to spend as much time there as I wanted, but one full day each week was to be taken off.

"On that day, put yourself in a neutral state of mind," said Rick. "No Kung-Fu at all."

On the free-practice days, a student may ask for advice from a higher-belt student, but questions must relate strictly to techniques pertinent to the enquiring student's belt level, and a student must not seek for extra knowledge. The same principle applies to the period before class, when students gather in the hall. Everyone is expected to keep busy, but during this time appropriate advice may again be sought from a higher-ranking student. Rick assured me that at the end of each class, Kai would remind us of one or two of the points we had just been discussing. He would make a different selection of points each time, and would add others, so that, over time, the key principles of behaviour and etiquette would become ingrained.

It was time to begin. The other twelve students were present, and Rick introduced me to Kai. He was about forty years old, stocky, with a powerful upper body and heavy legs. His thinning, jet-black hair was swept straight back, so that it seemed almost to be painted on. His eyes were set wide apart, which, combined with his severe hairstyle, gave him something of the sleek, brutal aspect of a large predator eyeing you up, more than a little forbidding. But this initial impression was quickly offset by his ready geniality, and a surprisingly open smile. He spoke in Chinese.

"Welcome. We are glad to have you in the class. Rick has given you an introduction, and I will go over the main points with you afterwards. But now we begin. Take your place beside Rick, and after the warm-up, he will give you an individual lesson. You will have individual lessons until you have been shown all the techniques required for your level. Then you can join the class for the whole period. Afterwards, you must practise the techniques you have learned. During class, you will also see some skills beyond your level, and you will be asked to practise some of these with a partner. But they are not yet your core knowledge. Get the feel of them when they arise, then leave them aside. Rick will teach you your core skills. And we will go from there."

The students stood in rows, facing Kai. We bowed, and began with circular rotations to stretch the back, twisting side to side, shoulder rolls, arm swings, and knee and head rotations. Then Kai called the horse stance. On the count, in unison, the high-knee raise and wide step brought us all into the stance, with Kai in front, looking like the bole of a massive deep-rooted tree. All around, each student also held the wide stance, everything correctly adjusted, centred as if by a plumbline.

The more I have studied, the clearer it is to me that when you acquire a skill by a great deal of patient effort, you recognise instantly another person who also has acquired that skill. Here, the camaraderie I instantly felt came straight from the body itself, in the shared knowledge of that stance. I suppose I felt a kind of pride. Kai had us hold the stance for ten minutes, and as the time ticked by and the legs began softly to burn, what I felt mainly was elation.

***

As I settled into my new training routine, the Art began also settling into me, ever closer to the centre of my everyday concerns. I was in my last year at school, and I was becoming increasingly indifferent to what I was learning there. But then, one of Kai's brief talks at the end of class reminded us that Kung-Fu should be grounded in a stable routine of daily life, and when he repeated this point a week or so later, I began to imagine that he might be directing his remarks specifically to me. I knew I was neglecting my schoolwork, and now I thought that I must change that, if only for Father's sake – and Uncle's. Still, in truth I was keen only to learn the Kung-Fu skills that Rick was teaching.

During the following months, I learned the six blocks, five horse stances, seven knife-hands, six elbows, three cat stances, three crane stances, the bow stance, high-back stance, low-back stance, half-moon stance, side-bow stance, broken bow stance, thrust punch, snap punch, backhand strike, hidden distance, nine different types of kicks – front, side, roundhouse, reverse roundhouse, spinning back, straight pushing, stiff swinging, rising, hooking – as well as four kinds of stepping.

These are the building blocks – the basic vocabulary that would be combined into phrases and sentences and then developed into persuasive, complex statements. I realized that 'the system', as Rick called it, would take years to master. He explained that the individual skills I was learning were part of a larger design, and by and by I would begin to feel something of that further pattern, so that a feeling of coherence would slowly grow and deepen. If there were only a collection of individual techniques, he said, then there could be no development. By contrast, the system provides a set of procedures, each of which backs up the others and is backed up by them, so that, in a stress situation, the system stands behind you – or, rather, is built into you – so that even a spontaneous reaction is guided, sometimes unconsciously, from within the larger internalised pattern. As Kai once said, "If you want to teach somebody nothing at all, then just teach them a great number of things all at once." What he meant is, an assortment of techniques – a collection of bits and pieces – is confusing and all but useless because there is no understanding of their interrelationship. Would you give a pile of bicycle parts – or, closer to the point, parts of several different bicycles – to someone who has never seen a bicycle, and tell them that they now have the equipment to ride safely down the street? No. And so, we learn a system because it is a dependable means of conveyance, as it were. Of course, there are many systems, a great many Kung-Fu 'styles'. What matters is that you choose one, and that it is properly taught.

Philippe's father visited Hong Kong twice between 1937 and 1938. The diaries provide a smattering of information about the visits, but Philippe was looking back from 1943 and did not intend to provide a close record of daily events. A few asides provide us with some hints:

'I remember Father and Uncle rattling on. The Chinese was quick. Never heard Father talk so much.'

'When Father walked into the Assembly Hall, everyone stared. He is elegant. Always looks as if he knows a great deal, but is keeping it to himself.'

'Uncle and Father in the library. They are a bat and ball – a tall, thin one and a small, round one.'

During the 1938 visit, Father and Uncle probably discussed Philippe's going into the jade business. As I have mentioned, the groundwork had been laid in the previous years, and Uncle had often talked to Philippe about jade. Also, Philippe's interest in Kung-Fu was connected from the start with his uncle's way of life, exemplified in turn by the house and its contents, so that the attractions of Kung-Fu were blended into and reinforced by the environment in which he lived.

It is not surprising, then, that Philippe found it an easy and pleasant transition from school to becoming an apprentice in Uncle's business. He was paid a small salary, which gave him some independence while reminding him of his responsibilities. Uncle had a network of clients in Europe, the United States, and Asia. He was also a regular at the great Hong Kong jade auctions, but he did not speculate in uncut jade. Rather, he was interested in antiques, and much of his collection was stored in warehouses. Rare items were placed in vaults, for security.

Uncle also owned a small, expensive store in the Mid Levels

on Hong Kong side, which he used mainly to meet clients who were interested in specialty items. The store was expensively appointed, with an office at the back furnished with antique mahogany throne-chairs and a grand table, inlaid with ivory and mother-of-pearl. The display cases were fitted with tooled brass locks and hinges, and the varnish, spotless glass, and perfectly adjusted lighting created an environment of discreet opulence, so that the store itself was a sample of the services and high quality merchandise that Uncle offered his clients. He also made detailed lists of his holdings, and one of Philippe's jobs was to design and produce catalogues, with illustrations, based on Uncle's lists. Philippe enjoyed the work because it was clearly defined, and also because of the beauty of the precious objects that he saw and handled every day.

When Philippe returned to Hong Kong after the war, to help Uncle to re-establish his business, he looked back upon what he had learned during his apprenticeship in 1938-39. Here is a diary entry, written in 1946, which I cite out of sequence because it is the only record of Philippe's appreciation and understanding of the precious materials with which he worked every day, before he had to flee Hong Kong because of the war.

DIARY AUGUST, 1946

Here I am, these years later, back in Uncle's world, the world of the markets and auctions, the rough-and-tumble trade that swirls about these wonders that he has collected with such pains, and which then move on as the buyers come and go. In returning, I can't help feeling the grief of so much that has been lost. The war changed everything. The stain reaches into every corner, and the wounds of the Japanese invasion have not closed and barely begin to heal. Yet, strangely, jade is more precious than ever, especially now as Uncle struggles to get his business up and running, to revive those ancient traditions of peace, harmony, and beauty so close to the heart of China itself.

Think of it. A history going back 8,000 years to the time before time when the Western Royal Mother – patron of jade carvers – instructed the Yellow Emperor in the arts of immortality. The old myths and legends console, more than I ever imagined before this war tore everything to shreds and extinguished the lives of countless millions. For Confucius, jade symbolises virtue, and through the ages it stands for the integration of heaven and earth. I think of the old names – Zingyan, Dushan, Lantian – and the characteristics of the stones they supply, the differences between degrees of purity and colour, sheen and lustre, the quite magnificent Hotan 'sheep-fat', the startling, brilliant Burmese jadeite. From Neolithic times, jade was a bridge between humans and the gods. It has been used in burials and cremations, rituals and divinations, for personal decoration and as a marker of social status. Each great dynasty made jade its own, so that the history of China and the history of jade are interwoven all the way back, speaking to us still through differences in openwork, relief, round carving, fretwork, enchasing, and in a dazzling variety of patterns – cloud and grain, double hooks, joined curves, fish scales, lozenges, whirlpools, tadpoles, silkworms, rush – these lead the eye in turn to the grain, sheen, texture, and the artful management and integration of imperfections and flaws. Veins and streaks might tell a story, enhance or blemish. The range of greens from apple to spinach, to grey-green and white, or with hues of yellow and red, violet and black, turned by the expert hand to a final result combining motif and design, colour and lustre, coarse or refined. A vast repertoire of motifs, opening everywhere upon myth, legend, and the joint-stock symbolism of the ancient culture – dragons and tigers, elephants, deer, unicorns, lotus flowers, peonies, peaches, geese, falcons, pomegranate petals and honeysuckle flowers, phoenixes, flying apsaras, fierce garudas, and meditating buddhas. Jade talks to us in a thousand voices. In its beginnings it was magic. It still is.

Philippe's understanding of jade had been expanded and deepened by his study of Asian antiquities at McGill University in Montreal, from 1942-45 – the years, that is, after he was sent back to Canada to escape the Japanese invasion of Hong Kong. The benefits of his education at McGill are also clear in the self-consciousness and persuasiveness of his writing, and in the fact that his diaries are often more than an occasional record of events and ideas. They frequently offer us Philippe's considered opinions, whether in what seem to be early drafts of university essays, or, later, in reflections on his reading, or explorations of ideas in the manner of a commonplace book or journal. But let us now move back to the point where his work in Uncle's business, as well as his Kung-Fu practice, were disrupted, and he was dispatched to Montreal.

In the happy period between, approximately, 1938 and late 1939, Philippe seems not to have realised how profoundly his Kung-Fu practice was influenced by the fact that in China the monasteries were under attack from both sides in the civil war. Buildings were destroyed, and monks were killed. Others fled, and those who belonged to the Shaolin Temple took with them the Kung-Fu traditions that had been cultivated in China for centuries. As with Buddhist monasteries in general, the Shaolin Temple was supported by the laity, whose patronage allowed the monks to maintain their contemplative way of life. But, as a result of the rending of the social fabric by the civil war and the Japanese invasion of China, monastic culture was all but destroyed, and the teachers who fled to Hong Kong found it impossible to maintain their traditional way of life. Some kept their knowledge of Kung-Fu to themselves; others tried to set up schools and to go on teaching in the right spirit, even in an environment that was not supportive of the monastic context out of which the teachings had grown. In some instances, less than scrupulous students and other opportunistic hangers-on freelanced in order to peddle a debased form of Kung-Fu, reduced to a set of street-fighting techniques. In the decades to come, so-called 'martial arts' would be exported to the United States, where they expanded rapidly in a highly commercialised form, though a number Shaolin masters also migrated there and continued to teach the authentic traditions.

As we see, Sifu was one of those who found a way to continue teaching in the right spirit, out of the public eye, as it were. I avoid using the word 'secret', here, because Shaolin Chan is not a cult, and, as with all genuine Buddhism, the core teachings are accessible and on offer to anyone. But when those teachings are transmitted through Kung-Fu, they need special protection against the all but endless mushrooming of violent martial-arts salesmen and glib pedlars of catchphrases drawn from Buddhist and Taoist wisdom traditions, all too often misappropriated and misused.

By contrast, in all its manifestations, from the basic techniques to the dynamism of the *kuen* and the stillness of meditation, the Art directs us beyond the illusions of the ego, beyond the three fires of greed, hatred, and delusion that the Buddha says we must strive to extinguish. No doubt this is why the person I am calling Philippe Ming wanted a story that would not focus on him, but, rather, as far as possible would be a witness to matters of broad human concern insofar as these can be revealed through Shaolin Chan Kung-Fu. And yet it is also the case that everyone is exposed to, and experiences, the seductions of the three fires, and this fact also has to be part even of a typical story, such as Philippe's, as we shall see. For now, let me return to the tradition of which Philippe had the good fortune to be a beneficiary.

I have been unable to discover many details about the Hong Kong school, except that it did indeed originate in the Shaolin diaspora from mainland China. It seems that Uncle facilitated the escape of Sifu and several other high-ranking monks, and, through his extensive connections in the Hong Kong business world, Uncle enabled Sifu to go on teaching. By and by, Sifu would return the favour, when it was Uncle's turn to flee from Hong Kong. Meanwhile, Uncle assembled a network of donors who felt as he did about the value of the Shaolin Chan heritage, and Sifu found himself supported by an endowment that generated enough income so that he did not have to worry about supplying his basic material needs, or those of his helpers. In return, Sifu established a discreet, carefully organised school. Recruitment was conducted with great care. Everything hinged on a prospective student's attitude and personal qualities, and athletic ability was a secondary consideration.

When Philippe began training, there were several groups of students, each group divided into classes – I have been unable to find the exact number. As students became more advanced, instruction became increasingly individual. For instance, not all of the advanced *kuen* were taught to every advanced student. Rather, a selection was made to suit a student's needs and aptitudes. This being the case, it is almost impossible to trace the identities and the training history of the most advanced practitioners. Indeed, because of the high value placed on anonymity, it is difficult even to find out who the high-ranking practitioners are.

As I have pointed out, special problems arise when Kung-Fu is disconnected from the monastic institutions within which it originated and was nurtured for centuries. But, also, as the historical record shows, the monasteries themselves were not exempt from problems. Consequently, it was perhaps inevitable that in Hong Kong Sifu should encounter his own set of difficulties, arising from within the school itself. For instance, not all students were discreet, nor did all students remain dedicated. Some left, and talked, and stories about Shaolin teachings began to circulate in Hong Kong and to get mixed into the muddle of martial arts teachings promoted by the usual array of entrepreneurs, as well as by criminal gangs interested in violent enforcement and intimidation. The most insidious of these gangs at the time were the organisations known as Triads. These were secret societies, bound by codes of behaviour, trained in the means of violence, and dedicated to goals that are the exact opposite of Shaolin ideals and values. Extortion, murder, exploitation, and profiteering from vice are the bread and butter of the Triads, even as their organisations are controlled and disciplined, calling, in their own way, for loyalty and anonymity. Not surprisingly, Triad members often studied martial arts. Wing Chun was favoured because it could be used effectively in alleyways, back rooms, hallways, even inside automobiles – the confined spaces where Triad gangsters often got on with their handiwork. The fact that Wing Chun was invented by a woman and named after a young girl whose name means 'flowering springtime' suggests something of the difference between the authentic Wing Chun and its sinister parody in the underground world of organised thuggery – a topic to which we will return by and by.

For now, suffice it to say that in the years between 1938 and 1939 Philippe lived securely within the embrace of his two apprenticeships – to his uncle, and to the best traditions of the Art. But the war in China was hurting Uncle's business in the East, just as the war getting underway in Europe was causing difficulties for him in the West. And so we return to the 1943 diaries, in which Philippe looks back in order to take stock of the key events that changed the course of his life in late 1939. These include the closing of Sifu's school, Uncle's flight from Hong Kong, and Philippe's return to Europe.

DIARY JULY, 1944

Late 1939 – things fall apart. 'Impermanence and sorrow', as Father says. I do not hang on to a re-imagined past in Hong Kong. That time is dead.

I remember noticing, first, that Uncle was worried. I thought it must be business. I knew there was trouble in China but I did not think that it was directly causing difficulties for him. I began to feel that something was wrong, not because he was becoming agitated, but because he was so much less agitated than usual. Being calm didn't suit him, and I even thought about asking him if there was some problem or difficulty with which I might help. Finally, one afternoon he told me, out of the blue, that movers would be coming the next day to pack some items in the house. We would be leaving temporarily, he said. Also, he had been in contact with Father during the past weeks, and had received news that he was now able to confirm through his own sources. We would have to act quickly, but things were going according to plan, and I should not worry. I was worried, of course, but Uncle asked me not to push for information just yet. He would get back to me soon.

I didn't see him for two days after that, but the packers turned up as he said. There were eight of them. They worked quickly, going methodically through the house and placing all the moveable objects into crates lined with straw and paper. The crates were then nailed shut and loaded onto trucks, and in a day and a half the job was finished. Some furniture remained, so that the house was functional, except that its treasures – its true inner life – were gone. I had no idea where, or why.

When Uncle turned up, he seemed, initially, more like his old self, but I expected he might be putting a good face on things.

"Apologies, dear Philippe. We are having an emergency. Quite a large emergency. I needed to let you know about the movers, and now I can tell you more. What I will say, you must keep to yourself. The Japanese will invade Hong Kong. You have heard rumours, and now I know that it will surely happen, perhaps any day. Your father has been able to determine that this is the case without doubt, and I have been able to confirm that what he says is true. But do not worry, you will be safe. Arrangements have been made – finalised just yesterday."

He paused, and the most I could do was to mutter, "The packing…?"

"Yes, I am going to store the whole collection. Everything valuable is going into crates, and within a few weeks most of it will be delivered to secure locations. A small amount will come with me. The shop also has been emptied and is being locked and boarded up – as if that will do any good, but who knows. Also, I have found a caretaker for the house."

"Where are we going? Are we going together?"

"We will travel separately. You must leave the day after tomorrow. A British naval transport aeroplane will take you to the west coast of Canada, to Vancouver. There will be several stops on the way, and you will change planes. I have papers for you, to carry with your passport. They confirm that you are an attaché, and you will in fact carry a pouch. Fake, of course, but entirely secure. You will be met in Vancouver, and then you take a train to Montreal. Your father is already there. So you must pack – one small suitcase, please."

My heart sank and I felt a sudden, surprising squall of pain and anger. I didn't want to be uprooted on a day's notice and dispatched to the far side of the world. Uncle picked up on my reaction.

"This is all very sudden, I agree. But we have been planning it for weeks, your father and I, as well as others. At first, the plan was only to have a plan in case we needed it. But things changed rapidly. The British troops here have no idea of the danger they are in. They should withdraw before the invasion starts. The Japanese will send an overwhelming force down through the New Territories. The – aptly-named – Gin Drinkers' Line won't hold, and its defenders will be annihilated. Your father knows this. And so we are in the calm before the storm, and we must take advantage before panic sets in. I have plans to leave shortly after you. I and the servants will travel together. We will be safe. And when it is all over, we will come back and start again. That is what

I hope, and also what I believe. So now, go and get ready. I must be off for the rest of the day, but I will go with you to the plane. It will be a shorter time of travel than your journey here. And, again, don't worry, everything is looked after."

"Can't I go with you?" I wasn't sure I did in fact want to go with him; it was just that I didn't want to leave at all, and this was the only thing that came to mind.

"It is not the plan," Uncle said, as if he were talking about divine dispensation. "You will come back when this is all over. And when this monstrous thing gathering in Europe is over. If the Japanese are mad enough to try to drive the Americans out of the Pacific, then the Americans will be involved and it will only be a matter of time. But there will be no end to the madness. We devour each other until we sicken. Then we fall asleep and call it peace. The Art knows about this, and teaches an understanding of it. So don't forget to keep up your practice, in whatever way you can. One day, you will begin classes again. Practise – even though you must do it by yourself."

***

And so, in late 1939 I came back here, to Montreal, to my grandparents' house. Father was at the train station to meet me. The Japanese of course did invade Hong Kong in 1941, and the British defences were overrun. A state of emergency was declared some time earlier, and, in mid-1940, the government issued an order for women and children to be evacuated. Uncle had correctly anticipated that disaster was imminent, and had acted to avoid the panic that prevailed six months after we left. I have no idea how bad things are in Hong Kong now, or what has happened to the people I knew. What has become of Leung, Kai, the people I saw every day in the markets, at school, the warehouse, the auctions, the great network of everyone living together – the network that you don't even know you are taking for granted until you lose it, until it is destroyed? A familiar grief comes again – loss without reason in a world where, as Uncle says, we devour each other. Father Time has iron teeth, and eats his children.

***

During the months after I came back, I got to know Father better than at any time before. As always, he was aloof – still the same tightly-rolled umbrella, with the same elegance and arresting presence. We talked, took walks, drank wine. I discovered that he was an excellent listener. Maybe I realised this because I had come, myself, to place a greater value on listening as a result of what the Art had taught me. Listening, after all, is a form of attention that decentres the ego by affirming the value of the other person. Without listening, nothing is learned. Without listening, there is no adequate response. Yet listening has to be learned as Kung-Fu is learned, and, in the end, the only way really to disarm violence is by dialogue. Violence occurs because dialogue fails, and dialogue fails because someone isn't listening. Like sparring, dialogue is an exchange between expert players, transcending egotism, transcending competition. High-ranking practitioners of the Art – I have seen this – can spar with extraordinary speed and power without doing one another the least physical harm. It is thrilling to watch. They make it look natural, spontaneous. By contrast, in a violent, physical confrontation, force is directed against an opponent in order to do harm. In Kung-Fu, we learn to deflect and return destructive energy to its source, so that the opponent might get the message: harm done rebounds upon the one who intends the harm.

Father knew these things, and because I was coming to recognise them myself, I was able to see that he knew. Perhaps this is why we talked more easily than before. Among other things, we discussed my flight from Hong Kong, and how I had been fortunate to get out. And, of course, I wanted to know about Uncle.

Father explained that Uncle and Sifu had left Hong Kong together, ten days or so after me. Uncle had been making preparations for weeks beforehand, and had, inconspicuously, been raising cash so that he could pay his way even if he were to be in exile for a number of years. Also, he had taken along a selection of precious jade. Many of the best carvings are small, and so he was able to carry a valuable treasure with him, as insurance. Otherwise, the bulk of his collection remained hidden in several locations, some in Hong Kong, some not. Now that the Japanese were in charge, Father had no reliable information about the condition of the house, or the store.

"Where did he go? And why Sifu?"

"Sifu and Uncle are closer than you might know. They are very old friends, dating back to when Sifu was still in the monastery. The civil war in China was very unkind to traditional monastic life, and since the 1930s, many monks have fled. Some came to North America, to San Francisco and New York, and also to Vancouver and even here, to Montreal. Among these were several Shaolin Grandmasters, preservers of the Art that you know about. Strange as it might seem, there are places now on this continent where the traditions of Shaolin Kung-Fu and the Chan Buddhism that underpins it, are more accessible than in China. There are a lot of imitators, but Sifu is the real thing. Uncle gave him protection in Hong Kong, and was able to find financial backers for the school you attended. The backers prefer to remain anonymous, as you might expect."

"And you are one of them," I said, suddenly clear about this.

"I am," Father replied, but then continued as if I had not asked, "and now that Uncle has had to flee, Sifu in turn has become his benefactor."

"So, they have gone back to China. Is that safe?"

"They have, and it is not safe. There is an old saying, that when things are bad in China, go to Hong Kong, and when things are bad in Hong Kong, go to China. At the moment, things are so much worse in Hong Kong that China is the better option. At first, they travelled by boat. Then there would be a long trek by jeep and horseback, into the mountains. They would need to know the movements of the Red and White armies, and the disposition of the local warlords. Their exact destination is not known to me, and so I can't tell you more, and perhaps it is best that way. But I do know that there are remote, abandoned monastic buildings and that Sifu has the connections to bring him to one of those. Safely, I hope. I imagine that we will be out of communication for as long as Uncle stays there."

"How will he live? What if the place is raided? Or if he gets sick?"

"The buildings are austere, true enough, and the terrain is difficult, but often it is beautiful – high stone escarpments, dense woods, veils of mist almost always hanging, drifting, suspended; a mysterious gauze curtain, a natural concealment. It is hard to grow enough to survive, but the small communities who have taken refuge there do their best. They are diligent and well organised. Rice and other staples – oil, nuts, seeds – as well as hand tools can be brought in small consignments, conveyed by trusted people. For the present, the locations are so remote and everything is so small-scale that no government official is likely to spend the energy and money that it would take to send soldiers to break up these few gatherings. And they would never find everyone, anyway. There are old Taoists living solitary lives in even more remote places. Sifu, together with a few of his closest followers, and Uncle, together with the servants from the Hong Kong house, made their escape together. I don't know if they will all travel to the same place – I very much doubt it – but everyone will be taken care of. Certainly Uncle and Sifu will stay with each other."

"What will happen now? How do we go on from here?"

"No one can say. In the world at large, things are terrifying.

All of Europe has entered into a nightmare, and in Asia – China, Japan, Korea – it is the same nightmare only with different sources. For my own part, I must be off to Europe very soon. I have been thinking that you might spend a year or two studying, here, at McGill University. You have a good preparatory education, and they will accept you." He tilted his head slightly to indicate that he had made the enquiries already. "You could study whatever you like – literature, oriental languages, antiquities, archaeology. Your grandparents are delighted to have you back, and they would love it if you would stay with them. Also, you can start practising again. You know the techniques, the basic forms. You have plenty to go on, now that you have been a student for, what, two years? Keep the knowledge alive. In return, it will give you life in unexpected ways."

This was my first clear indication that Father actually cared about my Kung-Fu. Also, with the story about Uncle and Sifu, I was beginning to see that the implications of the Art were more extensive than I had imagined. But mainly I was anxious about the future. As Father said, the war in Europe was terrifying, but to me it also seemed remote. Instead, my mind was on Hong Kong and China, and on the mist-shrouded hideaway where Sifu and Uncle were waiting things out. Their situation was more in my thoughts and brighter in my imagination than what was happening in Europe.

THE READER

In 1942, Philippe enrolled at McGill University, where he studied what might broadly be described as 'Oriental Antiquities'. Among other things, he took courses in Chinese calligraphy, and he learned to read Cantonese and Mandarin. These tasks required a great deal of patient memorisation, but by and by Philippe was able to decipher classical Taoist and Confucian texts, as well as Chinese poetry, folk tales, and some of the poetic but cryptic alchemical texts that were interwoven with ancient Chinese medicine. He read about Chinese history, and took the opportunity to learn about the Shaolin Temple, and about the blending of Taoist and Buddhist ideas in the development and practice of Chan. His enquiries led him also to the classical literature of Buddhism, which he read in the Theravada tradition through the Pāli Canon, as well as in a variety of Mahayana texts, especially Tibetan and Chinese. Among other things, the Chinese texts (many of which he read in translation) brought him back to his old friends the bodhisattva Kwan Yin and the redoubtable Ta Mo. His minor field of study was English literature, and he especially liked Shakespeare, Milton, and the Romantic poets.

The fact that Philippe was a student during the years between 1942 and 1945 helps to explain why the diaries begin in that period, when he had time to think and reflect. As a student, he was required to write essays, and sometimes he used his diaries to explore ideas and to shape his thoughts. Having to submit formal essays provided practice in writing and in the conduct of clear argument. The diaries during this period therefore provide a good deal of information about his broadening interests.

Still, the diaries do not mention that in 1943 Philippe moved into a student residence. University housing records confirm that he did so, and I have been able to discover that his education and accommodation were paid by his father, who also provided a monthly allowance. Philippe stayed in regular touch with his grandparents, but his father's comings and goings were intermittent, and Philippe did not see him for months on end. Then he would stay for a few days, perhaps a week. Philippe does not say if his father talked much about the war, but there are hints that he himself was disturbed by the course of world events. For instance, in 1944 he writes: 'The human race, insane – headlong in pursuit of its own destruction. Unbearable, disgusting. Deserved, I sometimes even think.' Again, in 1944, commenting on the Japanese bombing of Pearl Harbour in 1941: 'Uncle said it long ago – the Japanese might be foolish enough to attack the Americans. Well, "whom the Gods will destroy, they first make mad".'

But beyond a few notes such as these, the diaries do not dwell on the war, and perhaps Philippe focused on his studies as a way of taking his mind off the horrors delivered daily through the flickering newsreels, staccato radio broadcasts, and an endless flood of propagandist journalism. For our purposes, the main point is that during these years he supplied himself with a knowledge-base that remained indispensable during the rest of his life. His two fields of study – Asian Buddhism and Taoism on the one hand, and Western literature on the other – provided depth and range to the transcultural dialogue that had defined who he was from the start, and that would engage some of his best, most creative energies in the coming years.

The diaries do not say much either about Philippe's Kung-Fu in the years between 1942 and 1945, but it is clear that he continued to practise. A marginal note from 1943 reads: '40 mins. horse stance: took my eye off the clock, an eternity.' Later in the same year: 'Must note the difference the small room makes to the forms. You start taking your directions from the *shape of the room* and don't notice you are doing this until you try the same form in another place and find you are confused. Don't we in fact take directions all the time from the context, even if we are unaware of it?' And, from 1944: 'It came clear yesterday. The six blocks are of most use when they aren't blocking anything. Don't worry about fending things off; instead, guard the space. Then whatever comes at you won't matter.' Again, in 1945: 'Kai was right: what you have learned becomes part of you. But I need someone to take a look. There are details, things I've forgotten.'

Philippe seems to have practiced mostly in his room. Quite a small space – say, twelve by ten feet – would suffice, and if Philippe cleared his furniture out of the way, he would have more than that. Except for the long-fist forms, the *kuen* are by and large compact, going out and then facing square in another direction and ending up in the spot where the form began. Consequently, most of the *kuen* can be practised in a small area. Nonetheless, as far as Philippe's Kung-Fu is concerned, these years were a holding action, a maintenance of what he already knew. The great benefit was that the basic skills he had learned during the Hong Kong years became more deeply rooted than any student would achieve in a regular course of training. In short, Philippe's basic Kung-Fu became stronger than he himself realised.

A further point about the 1942-45 period is Philippe's relationship with a fellow student at McGill, whom I will call Elizabeth Bell. Several brief entries provide hints about their friendship. 'Meeting with L. today – I have learned the meaning of kenosis, and what Milton was thinking about.' 'Elizabeth B. sends invitation to P. Ming, with an inscription in Chinese, no less'; 'Liz thinks the Russians will invade Japan along with the Americans, and that it will be an impossible mess. It's already an impossible mess'; 'It occurs to me that when I fall into too much silence, I should see Liz. Chatterbox. Smart. Smartbox.'

There are various notes such as these, but no detailed information about what Elizabeth Bell meant to Philippe, or even how long he knew her. And so I thought to contact her, and, as it happens, it was not difficult to do. For most of her career, she had been a librarian at the University of Ottawa. She was still living in that city, and I thought of this as a lucky break. But the relative ease of access to Liz was offset by my puzzlement at what she told me, and which – with her permission – I have reshaped from the notes I jotted down after we talked.

First, I sent Liz a short letter of introduction to say that I thought she might like to know that Philippe Ming had died. I explained that I was a personal friend, and I gathered that she had known him at McGill in the early 1940s. I was preparing an obituary memoir, and any recollections she might have would be helpful. She replied promptly, and we agreed to meet in the Ottawa University library. There would not be many people in the reference room, and she would wear a red scarf.

And so we met, and moved to a nearby café to talk. On the way, I spoke about Philippe to confirm that I was well enough informed about him for my interest not to be trivial. And, of course, I was also trying to make some assessment of her. She was of medium height, thin, with slightly protuberant eyes and a broad forehead. Her hair was tied back into a bun, which made her look severe, but her face was engagingly mobile when she spoke. She was alert, and, when the conversation got going, she was quick and vivacious. She asked for information about Philippe's death, and I told her as much as I knew. He was a teacher, I said, of a specialised form of Buddhism, to which he had devoted his life. It is called Chan, and I was his student. He taught the physical exercises connected to the practice of the particular branch of

Chan in which he specialised, and which derives from what is known as Long-Fist Kung-Fu. For the most part, he did this in Hong Kong.

Liz said that she knew that Philippe had studied Chinese Buddhism and Taoism, and she wasn't surprised that he had pursued what was for him such a passionate interest. She knew also that he was fascinated by the comparisons and contrasts between what he found in the Buddhist sutras and English literature. For a while, he had been interested in the great English epic poem, *Paradise Lost*. The Buddha and Milton were revolutionaries, he had said, despite how differently they saw the world. The overlaps and contradictions, the unexpected interdependencies between contemplation and action, acceptance and protest, resignation and rebellion that Philippe found in these two great figures intrigued and puzzled him, and he talked about such things a great deal. He was gentle and sensitive, Liz went on, but there was also a certain anguish about him, and he was drawn to the Buddhist sutras and to *Paradise Lost* because the Buddha and John Milton alike had set out to give an answer to the problem of suffering that Philippe always felt so deeply.

When I asked if there were any personal details that might help me to understand Philippe better, Liz was, again, forthcoming. "He and I talked quite a lot. We spent a lot of time with one another, but we weren't, as you might say, 'going together'. There was something inaccessible about him – something guarded. And then he told me about his mother, and that was when I felt I really came to know him. To be honest, I was not keen on getting myself into anything emotionally complex. We all have our stories. Anyhow, he told me that his mother had abandoned him when he was a baby, and he never did find out where she went. His father has remained distressed to this very day, Philippe said, but still his father held out hope of discovering where she was. For his part, Philippe did not expect that to happen, but he kept a spark of hope alive, for, who knows, isn't the world full of surprises? Philippe's father had a business in Hong Kong, buying and selling antiques, and he travelled a lot. According to Philippe, travelling allowed his father to keep searching, but he was a lost soul, and what he tried to pass off as business travel was really an expression of grief and heartbreak. For his own part, Philippe was studying at McGill with a view to eventually going into antiques himself. He didn't need an academic qualification to do so, but his father's business was at a standstill because of what was happening in Hong Kong, and being a student was a good way to learn about ancient Chinese culture. In turn, such knowledge would be an asset when he took up his chosen line of work. Philippe said also that his father was arranging a traditional Chinese marriage for him, and although Philippe was not sure that it would work out, he would wait and see. He believed that his father wanted something more secure for his son than had turned out to be the case for himself when he broke with tradition and married a Westerner. Surely there would be no point in making his father feel worse by refusing to agree to an arrangement that was far from being made and might in fact never be made.

When he told me these things, his candour was touching. He was perhaps more of a wounded warrior like his father than he thought. And so we were friends, but we had a sort of tacit agreement that the world was making different claims on us. After he graduated and went back to Hong Kong, we sent letters to each other for a while, but eventually the correspondence petered out, and then stopped. I went on to study library science, and I had my own adventures. I did not hear anything more about Philippe until you made contact."

I had hoped that Liz might help me to fill out the picture of Philippe's student days, and up to a point she did. But of course she made that picture a great deal more complicated. Why had he lied to her? Or was she remembering incorrectly? Or was there perhaps more to their relationship? When she first told me what Philippe said about his mother, I was uncomfortable, but I backed away from pressing the matter any further. Afterwards, I thought about asking to meet again, so that I could clear the air. But what good would it do to tell Liz that Philippe had lied about his mother, his father, and himself? I was prepared to forget the whole episode, and, even, not to include it here. But as the narrative of the diaries increasingly took shape in my mind's eye, Liz's recollections began to make sense, as we shall see.

So far, I have mentioned that the diaries written during the Montreal years contain only scattered references to the war, and that they provide quite a lot of information about Philippe's broadening interests. The big ideas that he was exploring as part of his education in fact make up the bulk of the entries. And so I now present a selection of passages written in 1944, over a period of several months. In general, I have arranged my selection in the interests of thematic continuity, and in so doing, I have not always followed the exact chronological order of composition.

DIARY APRIL-OCTOBER, 1944

University – not like school, but a chance to find out rather than be told. I will never look at an algebra problem again, but I will throw myself forever into these old books, these amazing, astounding antiquities.

***

How fascinating, that so many of the classic texts pass back through legend into myth, poised at the edge of timelessness, yet making a historical claim. The Yellow Emperor, Lao Tzu, the Western Great Mother – these begetters of tradition before there was a tradition, the mysterious origins written over and written over again, expanded, deepened by the gathering wisdom of an awakening knowledge of what it means to have a history, to be in history.

The Shamans, pre-historical mediators between the people and the heavens, wandered amongst the stars and walked the ritual dances to heal the sick, to drive away demons, in a trance embracing and embraced by the vibrations of the Tao, the great dynamic equilibrium in which we dwell and which dwells in us. Those old magicians, their dances are also the beginning of Kung-Fu. Today there are Shamans in Siberia, in Mongolia. If I visited, what would I say?

***

The ancient voices of the Shamans can be heard echoing still in Lao Tzu, most revered of the old Taoist sages, most translated, most read. His wise man is immune to poison, talks to animals, knows the techniques for prolonging life. These are traces, ghosts from the deep time of the star-travellers. But Lao Tzu's thinking and the beautiful construction and patterning of his metaphors also belong to a different world, a world of high self-consciousness and power of analysis. Yet, the Shamans remain the wellspring, the deep source.

Lao Tzu's main point: the energy of the cosmos, the stuff of the stars, of the universe, is the stuff of ourselves. To live well is to dwell consciously in this glorious play of energies making up the universe and ourselves together, that he calls the Tao. Straight away then he tells us that the Tao that can be named is not the Tao. He repeats this throughout in different ways, directing us again and again through language beyond language: 'Those who know do not talk. / Those who talk do not know'. I hear Uncle saying that those who know about Kung-Fu don't talk about it, and those who talk about it don't know.

For Lao Tzu, the Tao spills out of itself, as it were, to become the 'ten thousand things' of the world, a great emanation that is then gathered in again to its beginning, as the 10,000 things return to their source. This expression and return, activity and yielding, is called male and female, yang and yin. To be human is to engage with the world of the 10,000 things and to 'achieve results', take initiatives and deal with problems – if possible, before they happen – but without pursuing praise or honour, which are imposters. Rather, getting your self out of the way is the gateway to the Tao. In turn, being open to the source, to receptivity, to yielding, is to know the mysterious female, the 'valley spirit'. 'Know the strength of man, / But keep a woman's care! / Be the stream of the universe'. So, we are to engage the world, but also we are to understand that yielding is more powerful than force. 'Under heaven nothing is more soft and yielding than water / Yet for attacking the solid and strong, nothing is better.' Lao Tzu writes a lot about the mother, silence, water, emptiness, and how to act by way of non-action. This is not easy to understand, but not understanding it is also the point. The mysterious female remains a mystery, an absence that I dream of making present, that I desire to make present and that I don't know how to make present. The presence of the absence is perhaps the point?

Lao Tzu, the 'Old Fellow', knew all about the difficulties of living, learning, understanding. 'Accept misfortune as the human condition', he says, because misfortune 'comes from having a body'. The central fact again: we suffer unaccountably, and this being so, Lao Tzu insists that there is no greater misfortune than wanting something for yourself, because 'he who grasps loses'. And yet, he says, we are to be vigilant in order to avoid 'underestimating the enemy'. Today, amongst the clashing armies, invasions, fire-storms and mass destruction, what does it mean not to desire something, to yield, and yet not to underestimate the enemy?

***

The Holy Trinity of ancient Taoism – Lao Tzu, Chuang Tzu, Lieh Tzu. The same message with variations, three different voices. Ah, the voices! But were these old writers actual people? There are different theories. Still, it is clear that a body of wisdom was gathered and passed by word of mouth for centuries before it was gathered again to be written down. By whom? Mostly, we don't know, but, then, this is the way with all the classics at the start of the great cultural traditions beginning around the fifth century BC – in Greece, India, Israel, as well as China.

***

Chuang Tzu, a thorn in the side of respectable moralists, a satirical outsider who fills his book with crazy people – the maimed, wounded, discarded, reviled. In the eyes of the world, Chuang Tzu tells us, the sage seems stupid and the good man crazy. And so we need to look again at the conventional judgements that close us off inside a world that we are mostly busy trying to make comfortable for ourselves. By contrast, the wild energy of the Tao brings a freedom of radical insecurity, which means embracing whatever we have reviled in our efforts to make ourselves safe and comfortable. All things are alike in the Tao, and 'in their difference is their completeness; / in their completeness is their difference'.

There is a lot of laughter in Chuang Tzu. Self-righteousness does not stand up well to laughter. But there is a lot also about skill, and there is a method in Chuang Tzu's madness. For instance, Lord Wen Hui admires the great skill of an ox butcher who explains that he loves the Tao. For him this means that over many years he has learned to butcher an ox so that his knife glides effortlessly and he doesn't have to think about it as the blade passes without resistance between the spaces of the joints. In another place, a swordsmith answers the Grand Marshal who asks 'Do you have the Tao?' The swordsmith replies, 'I do have the Tao', and by this he means that he has concentrated so hard on making swords that he is 'able to do it without thinking'. How often have I heard the same thing from Leung and Kai. Practice should become a habit so ingrained that it turns into a natural expression of the body. Chuang Tzu calls this 'actionless action'. 'Remain sure in actionless action, and all things will transform themselves. Reject your body, throw out hearing and eyesight, forget that you are anyone, become one with the vast and the void'. And so the Art takes you over and you are in the Tao, like the butcher and the swordsmith. The perfect man leaves no trace, says Chuang Tzu, because whatever he does is not about him, not about his ego, and when you describe him you are talking about his 'unity with the great All', and 'the great All has no self'.

True: the Art takes you out of yourself, and yet the world claws you back, and there is a lot in the world that you cannot just laugh off. 'There is no one thought more of by all generations than the Yellow Emperor', Chuang Tzu writes, yet even the Yellow Emperor could not prevent war, and when he fought on the battlefield 'the blood flowed for a hundred miles'.

The third great classic is the book of Lieh Tzu, who steadies us, as Chuang Tzu alarms us. In contrast to that old eccentric, Lieh Tzu is humdrum. In Lieh Tzu, we meet the 'Mysterious Female' again, but her mystery now is toned down, and, for the most part, she is a useful antidote to everyday anxiety, because strength needs to be 'complemented by softness' and 'if you resist too much, you will break'. Lieh Tzu tells us also about a fisherman and a charioteer, who, like Chuang Tzu's butcher and swordsmith, acquire their skill patiently, so that it is exercised by second nature. But for Lieh Tzu the special skill lies in not being exceptional, and he sees his ordinary day-to-day fallibilities as a protection against vanity. 'Someone who is enlightened does not appear perfect', he writes, but even enlightenment is not all that exceptional, or mysterious. Rather, it is 'a very normal experience, attainable by everyone', as long as you don't let your ego get in the way. We are all travellers, and in a world where everything changes, the beginning of wisdom is the acceptance of imperfection.

***

The powerful meeting between Taoism and Buddhism. The place: The Shaolin Temple.

***

Gautama Siddharta – Buddha. His message came to China around the first century AD, and seems to have arrived by way of Tibet. From the start, the Shaolin Temple was Buddhist, built at the end of the fifth century and devoted to the translation of Buddhist texts into Chinese. The translations have a Chinese flavour because Taoist language was used for many Sanskrit terms. Then came Bodhidharma – Ta Mo – the gruff old wayfarer I first met when Uncle explained his statue in the hallway of the Hong Kong house. As it turns out, Ta Mo is at the heart of the story, because he founded what we now call Shaolin Chan. This supposedly occurred in AD 520, at the temple in Hunan, in Northern China, but, as with the old Taoists, a lot remains obscure. For instance, the writings of Ta Mo are handed down for the most part indirectly, and there aren't many of them. But the legends about him are lively, and plentiful. They tell how the ragged old hobo made his way to China from Southern India, perhaps along the Silk Road. He began as a student of Prajnatara, whose unconventional, mind-to-mind transmission of Buddhism appealed to his disciple, whose own interpretation became known in China as Chan – later developed in Japan, as Zen.

When Ta Mo initially was refused entry into the Shaolin Temple, legend has it that he sat in a cave for nine years, staring at the wall and meditating. There is even a story that he cut off his eyelids to enhance the concentration of his gaze. But, as Uncle explained long ago, 'wall-examining' is a way of describing how meditation blocks out distractions. Don't we still say, 'keep your eyes peeled' when we mean 'pay careful attention?'. Anyhow, Ta Mo's fierce patience made such an impression that after all it seemed not such a bad idea to let him into the temple – which he then transformed.

For Ta Mo, 'self and other' are identical, but each of us has to discover this alone. There is no method for learning how to do such a thing, and it is best not even to seek to learn. Worldly people 'are in a perpetual state of delusion,' we are told, and in the Dharma 'there is no self'. Only by seeking nothing are we liberated, and so 'there is nothing that is practiced'. As with Lao Tzu, language here again is pushed to its limits to show that language does not bring us all the way. The main thing is to meditate and find out for yourself. Meditation, however, does not consist in just sitting. As Uncle also said, legend has it that Ta Mo introduced physical exercises to the Shaolin Temple. This was probably for the health of the monks, but also as a way of enabling them to understand how movement can also be meditation. Were these exercises a form of Hatha Yoga, as might seem likely? Who knows? But it is certain that they were not the martial-arts teachings developed at the Shaolin Temple some 700 years later. Still, the spirit of Shaolin remains to this day the spirit of Ta Mo's Buddhism.

But why martial arts in a monastery? Health and fitness, yes. Perhaps for defence against bandits? Or because the monks were called to protect the empire? Or because, in the enduring image of the irrepressible Ta Mo, physical stress and the danger of violence in combat can themselves become a meditative exercise designed to transcend the ego at the point where the ego is most likely to want to protect itself. In practising the forms, you are not there, Kai said. The Art takes you out of yourself. It is a moving meditation that remains undisturbed, even under stress.

***

Taoism, Confucianism, Buddhism – the core systems of old China. I am getting a picture. If you start down that road, you can go on for a lifetime.

***

In our study of the foundations of Buddhism, we are reading the Pāli Canon – or parts of it. The first authoritative, deliberately assembled collection of Buddhist scriptures, translated in Ceylon in the first century before Christ, it is as close as Buddhism gets to an official body of texts. Its authority is greatest in the Theravadan countries that make up one of the two great Buddhist families. Chinese Buddhism belongs in the other family, the Mahayana. Beginning with the Pāli Canon gives you a good grasp of the Buddha's story and his core teachings. Then you can see how these play through all the varieties of Mahayana.

***

The problem of suffering is there from the start. Gautama Siddhartha was a well-off young prince. He married at sixteen, and had a son. He was rich, privileged, content, but he was not supposed to leave the palace, so that he would remain protected from the evils of the world. One day, however, he went outside, and he saw a lame man, an old man, and a corpse. Now the problems of sickness, age, and death were stuck in his head. And with them came the question: How do we escape from suffering?

***

Gautama's first step in pursuit of an answer was to leave his wife and child and become an ascetic, testing the limits of self-denial. But that produced only more grief, and he relented, nourished himself, and kept searching. Then, one day as he sat meditating under a tree, it came to him. Enlightenment. Nirvana.

As usual, the trouble with enlightenment – as with the Tao – is that you can't describe it. It is beyond language and even beyond experience because there is no separate self to have an experience. At first, the Buddha thought he would spend his life alone, meditating, but the god Brahma convinced him to spread the word and to teach others. And yet, because nirvana can't be described, wouldn't any teaching of it give the wrong idea? What, then, do we make of the fact that the Pāli Canon is filled with rules, prohibitions, instructions, exhortations, all manner of intricate classifications? It is thick with them, thousands of pages, hugely invested in language. Shouldn't all that be beside the point? 'You should live as islands unto yourselves,' says the Buddha, 'being your own refuge, with no one else as your refuge.' That is what Ta Mo also says.

One answer is, in a word, 'compassion'. Without it, there is no Buddhism. Gautama agreed to teach in order to help others to become liberated from suffering, and one of his main ideas is that we are bound together in a vast chain of cause and effect reaching across the aeons – the 'Chain of Dependent Origination'. In meditation, perhaps indeed we are islands unto ourselves, but then out of compassion we engage again with the needs of others. This is what the Buddha did through his long preaching career, during which he constantly adjusted his message to the capacity of his listeners, using various kinds of 'skillful means' to help to bring them to the moment of realisation that, in itself, can't be described.

And so, the Buddha's first sermon in the deer park got his teaching under way, and in it he sets out the four Noble Truths

– the Truth of Suffering, the Origin of Suffering, the Ending of Suffering, the Path Leading to the Ending of Suffering. Mainly, he wants to say that the ending of suffering occurs only when selfish concerns are abandoned. Later, in his Fire Sermon, he describes the three fires – hatred, greed, delusion – that fuel the cravings that, in turn, are the root cause of suffering. Finally, he sets out the Noble Eightfold Path as a plan for extinguishing the three fires. The elements of the Noble Eightfold Path are analysed frequently, often in great detail. However, the Pāli Canon comes to life, not in these analyses, but in the Buddha's engagements with actual people. There, he can be philosophical, inventive, ironic, indirect, persuasive, aggressive, even sometimes threatening. His exchanges are like sparring, and often he returns the negative energy directed against him, back to its source. For instance, at one point he summons a demon to threaten the rude and insulting Ambattha, and the demon threatens to split Ambattha's head into seven pieces if Ambattha can't behave better. And so the path to the ending of suffering lies not just through a retreat into meditation. For the Buddha, the path also means being engaged with the world and with others.

Too bad, that the Pāli Canon doesn't deal with the bodhisattvas, who are of special interest in the Mahayana. A bodhisattva – such as Kwan Yin – refuses to escape the wheel of rebirth, but chooses to return, until the suffering of every sentient creature is relieved. Uncle introduced me to that idea in Hong Kong. Father Gilles in Montreal said Jesus suffers for us all and the only god worth believing in is the one who suffers alongside us.

The most important conversation of all, then: between Jesus and the Buddha. The Buddha sits in meditation. He is a triangle with its base on the ground – stable, balanced, harmonious. Jesus is crucified. He is a triangle with its apex on the ground – unstable, precarious, agonised. Are these opposites, or the same thing viewed the other way around? Together, aren't they a star, in the shape of the Wisdom of Solmon?

***

I hadn't realised: in the New Testament, many books could have been chosen instead of those four, the Gospels. The key point is that the main contenders, the so-called 'gnostic' books, do not put Jesus's death at the centre, as the Gospels do. By contrast, St Paul says 'Christ and him crucified' is all he knows, and the way that leads beyond suffering is to follow Jesus even if that means following him into fear, horror, death. This is a tragic vision, and Christianity doesn't trust anyone who doesn't have a tragic view of life. How many Christians know this? It is too terrifying, dangerous, extreme, and the only thing then that keeps you from despair is faith that love can do better, can bring about the kingdom, a real communion in contrast to the parody-communities shaped by the violence, greed, and oppression that history goes on delivering. Of all the great religions, Christianity forces this question on us the most unflinchingly. How do we affirm a god who stage-directs the human tragedy?

For the Buddha, God's existence is an open question about which it is better not to be concerned. If a man is struck by an arrow will he be preoccupied with who shot it, what kind of bow was used, or how the bow was strung? The main thing, says the Buddha, is to remove the arrow and to heal the wound. So, the question of God's existence is not as important as getting rid of suffering.

But Jesus was a prophet in the Hebrew tradition. He had a revolutionary vision, and he wanted to be on the side of the outcast, the despised, the homeless, when the revolution occurred. The last book of the New Testament describes that time. The Book of Revelation is the opposite of the patient, suffering Jesus who is a scapegoat victim. It is not gentle, or accepting, or personal.

Instead, it is impersonal, violent, dangerous. And so there is only one way to read it that makes sense in relation to the Gospels. It is about how the crucifiers of Jesus bring their own destruction on themselves. At the end of history, the tyrants are annihilated by their own actions, by what they have let loose. As Kai kept saying, in Kung-Fu one main idea is to realise that you can turn a harmful attack directed at you back to its source, because, by and by, the cosmic karmic process will do that in any case.

As I have mentioned, the ideas that Philippe was exploring in these excerpts remained fundamental throughout his career. His Kung-Fu practice continued to be underpinned by the Taoism and Buddhism about which the 1944 diaries tell us. And the relationship between Christianity and Buddhism that he explored in some depth at McGill exerted a profound influence that helped him to manage his own indignation and resentment – the personal 'black dog' that had accompanied him since his mother's death, and that remained a linchpin in the narrative of his life.

THE GROUP OF FIVE

In 1946, Philippe returned to Hong Kong. His uncle had arrived back shortly after the war, and was keen to get his jade business up and running. He felt that if he could re-establish his international connections quickly, he would be ahead of the slowly reviving, post-war market. In general, he had found the Hong Kong business world in tatters, not least because regulations were often ignored or were not enforceable. This, in turn, left the way open for criminal gangs, such as the Triads, to run protection rackets, loan-sharking operations, as well as gambling, prostitution, drugs, and smuggling. In this situation, Uncle decided that the safest thing to do would be to attend first to his international trading partners.

When he returned to Hong Kong, Uncle still had most of the jade that he had taken with him to China, but the bulk of his inventory remained in the hidden locations where he had left it, and it would have to be discreetly recovered, over time, and safely stored. For now, because of the widespread post-war insecurity, he decided to let his hidden jade remain hidden. In his absence, the store had been broken into and vandalised. The house had fared better because it had a caretaker, and because it was neither a benefit nor a cause of concern to the Japanese. Nonetheless, it had become run-down. There were problems with the gutters and roof tiles, and there was water damage. First, Uncle wanted to get the store fixed up and made secure, and then repair the house. But to do these things, he needed money.

As far as I have been able to discover, a bank financed him, with the house as security. But Uncle had other plans that a bank-loan wouldn't cover. Sifu and a small number of those close to him had also returned to Hong Kong, and Uncle wanted to re-establish the school as soon as possible. He did not convey to Sifu that money was short, but he knew – despite his own misgivings – that he would need to sell some jade straight away, perhaps on the black market.

I have no idea how Uncle made contact with the underground economy, but he knew a lot of people in the business world, and, probably, the right introductions led him to Wang Pak, a black-market entrepreneur. Uncle of course knew the value of what he had for sale, but was surprised when Pak offered him a good price straight off. "A fair price," Pak said. "As you know. Take the offer, and if you need me to help you again, I am here. I want to look after your interests."

And so, Uncle took the money and got on with his plans. The great Hong Kong auction houses were struggling, and there was very little local trade in the kind of high-end jade in which he specialised. Also, trade with China was virtually at a standstill, and so Uncle focused on the Middle East, South East Asia, as well as New Zealand, Canada and Indonesia. As it turned out, things went well, and during the following year profits began to pick up.

During that time, the loan from Pak paid for the house repairs and refurnishing, and Uncle also rented and furnished a second house, together with a disused storage facility, both of which Sifu could adapt to the needs of the school. Philippe would soon be returning to Hong Kong to assist in the business, and no doubt Uncle expected that Philippe would resume his training with Sifu.

For his part, after Philippe finished his studies at McGill in late 1945, he was, for a few months, employed in an immigration office, helping to promote Canada as a destination for migrants, mostly from Europe. In the post-war period, the British Government provided assisted passage, with the idea of supplying countries such as Australia, New Zealand, and Canada with new arrivals who would preserve British values and a British way of life. French Canada was as keen likewise to preserve French values, and Philippe was kept busy, especially with immigrants to Quebec. Then, in the summer of 1946, his father relayed the news that Uncle was safely returned to Hong Kong and had asked if Philippe would like to go back to help with the business. Philippe leaped at the opportunity, and, late in 1946, he set out again on the long journey. He must have realised that things augured well – his knowledge of Chinese had improved greatly, and he had learned a lot about Chinese history and antiquities, which would complement his already sound basic knowledge of the jade business. Also, he had kept up his Kung-Fu practice, and he looked forward to starting in the new school, about which he had also been informed.

And so, in early 1947, Philippe became one of a small group of five students who were selected as part of Sifu's new enterprise. Kai was no longer teaching, and there were two new chief instructors. The training hall was a converted storage room situated on the border of the old Walled City. It had been part of a furniture manufacturing business, and the offices upstairs were being used as a sewing machine repair shop. The general area round the Walled City was run-down, but the storage room was made secure and the interior was refurbished and well-appointed. The shabby outside appearance was left as it was, in order not to attract attention. The training hall was less than a half-hour walk from the small house in which Sifu and the instructors lived, on the other side of Nathan Road. Several rooms in the house were set apart for meditation, forms practice, and private instruction. As always, great care had been taken with the selection of students. In Philippe's class, all five had been members of the pre-war school, though Philippe was acquainted with only one of them. Still, their meeting felt like a reunion.

Philippe, of course, did not realise that Uncle was financially over-extended, and, to the best of my knowledge, Sifu had no idea either. Before the war, benefactors had been easier to find. Now, by and large, prospective donors were short on funds, and were less inclined in any case to be involved with martial arts. Hadn't they seen enough of that? And so, probably within a year after Philippe's return, Uncle found himself paying another visit to Pak. I expect that Pak was not surprised. During their first meeting, he had acted generously, no doubt as an inducement, and he had invited Uncle to return.

Although I never met Pak, I have seen photographs of him in the Hong Kong papers, taken shortly after he was arrested in 1951 and also during his trial. He was in his mid-fifties, squat and dense, like a bollard, both fat and strong, and with short, heavy legs. His shoulders looked surprisingly narrow, given his bulky arms, so that he had something of the appearance of an over-fed penguin. He wore glasses with round black rims, and his thick glossy hair was tied back into a ponytail. He had rings on both hands, and from under the tight white shirt collar at the side of his neck appeared a tattoo, which, I imagined, would extend down his back. He was not exactly an appealing sight – a combination of the repellent and the arresting, definitely more toad than prince.

On Uncle's second visit, Pak agreed to buy more jade on condition that he could insure Uncle's business. After all, Hong Kong was unruly, and Pak would guarantee to keep Uncle's properties safe, together with their contents. The premium would be a modest percentage of Uncle's profits, and, because these were just beginning to rally, the service would be free until the business got on its feet. Meanwhile, Pak would buy jade for cash, and they would have a gentlemen's agreement about the insurance for two years, after which they could reconsider.

Uncle was shrewd and must have realised that he was buying protection, but he went ahead anyway. Perhaps the Triad you know is better than the Triad you don't. However, when I consulted the press archives and talked to people who remembered the trial, I began to see that Uncle's motives were complex, and that in fact he was playing Pak as much as Pak was playing him. Uncle needed cash. Also, he knew that word would get about in the Hong Kong underworld that his business was under Pak's protection, and no one would interfere if he discreetly transferred his hidden treasures to his warehouses or to the market – the black market, if necessary. But why would Uncle take such a risk? The short answer is that he had a long-term plan, part of which was, simply, that he counted on Pak's greed to bring about Pak's undoing. However, Uncle's plan would soon run into a major problem that he could not have foreseen, and that almost derailed it altogether, as we shall see.

During 1947 and 1948, as Uncle's business grew, Pak made sure that the best safes, doors, and window bars were installed, without compromising the elegance of Uncle's posh Mid-Levels establishment, and, most important, he provided security in insecure times. But then, in 1948, he requested that his own auditors oversee Uncle's books, and, for this service, he charged Uncle exorbitant accounting fees. Also, in 1948 he billed Uncle for the safes and refurbishments. For now, he would take jade in place of cash, but he insisted on selecting pieces of much greater value than the amounts that he was owed. When Uncle protested, Pak pointed out that he was doing Uncle a favour by not demanding cash, and by allowing Uncle to reinvest his profits, which were already on the rise thanks to Pak. During this time, Uncle found it increasingly difficult to get direct access to Pak, and had to deal instead with his henchmen. In short, Pak was now showing his hand as an extortionist, and yet, without him, Uncle's business and Sifu's school would probably not have survived in the early post-war years.

To prevent Philippe from coming into contact with Pak or his unpleasant helpers, Uncle had arranged for Philippe's work to be done either in the warehouses or at home. Boxes of files were moved into the library, on the grounds that it was well equipped with most of the reference books that Philippe needed for the purposes of cataloguing and of assessing provenance and value. To Philippe it did not appear that he was being steered away from the store, and he enjoyed his work, suspecting nothing – at least initially.

The other main aspect of Philippe's life between 1946 and 1950 was, of course, Kung-Fu, and, with his four companions, he was heavily engaged in an intense training programme, which had the additional effect of shifting his attention away from Uncle's business on Hong Kong side. The diaries during these years deal mostly with Philippe's progress in the Art, and he kept a detailed written record, probably in order to help himself to organise and assimilate the large amount of new knowledge he was receiving, as the following selection of excerpts shows. In addition, the excerpts contain some interesting reflections on his first impressions on his return to Hong Kong.

DIARY DECEMBER, 1946 – JANUARY, 1950

How different, how impossibly not-the-same as Canada. There, the vastness, the immense wildernesses, endless skies, endless snows. Here, the endless crowds, labyrinths of streets, hubbub, clamour.

***

Uncle, scuttling about. The old house is run-down and being repaired – new roof, pilasters, paint. This is happening all over Hong Kong.

***

Uncle is drumming up old contacts. "Trying to be ahead of the game," he says. I am to get on with the catalogues. Soon the warehouses will reopen.

***

The beauty of jade, now that I see it again and hold it to the light. A songbook of colours and textures, and the music of the songs is the music of old China; the more enchanting the more you know and understand. These deep greens and grey-greens, hues of white, pink, violet, red and black – a waking dream. Greens that are emerald, spinach, apple, lighter or darker, speckled or veined, and with a depth deeper than the deepest place of your heart or mind, yet shining, clear. But isn't beauty a distraction, and is there any other God, after all, than death?

***

I have been finding out about the Japanese in 1941. The British and Canadians offered resistance, but were overwhelmed and killed or captured and sent to labour camps where many more died. Thousands in Hong Kong were murdered, including patients bayoneted in their beds in St Steven's Hospital. Thousands of girls were destroyed. And so Hong Kong fell, and fell to pieces. In mainland China, the siege of Nanking was as bad as the worst that happened here, or anywhere. I have imagined, and after the horror of discovery comes anger. Vengeance. It is in our blood. Yet Jesus and the Buddha say no. I have seen photos of the shells of the burned out cities. There are no photos of the hundreds of thousands of people burned to death or half-burned or flayed and blinded by the blast and left half-alive by the atomic fire storms. We do this because we are human.

***

The new school is in two locations. The training hall is a converted storage room. It is in a rough part of Kowloon, but there is also a house, in a separate location, for private instruction. I met Sifu at the house this morning, with four other students. He looked exactly the same. In his traditional Chinese gown he reminded me of a willow or a silver birch; lithe, but steady. He explained that the five of us were selected for an intense programme of instruction and practice.

We all had received our basic knowledge before the war, and our skill levels were roughly equivalent. We had kept up our practice, and without that we would not be here, Sifu said. But, today he wanted to ask for a commitment. If anyone had reservations, these would be respected and there would be no problem about leaving. A note or a private word would suffice if we wanted to withdraw, but he asked that we decide before things got under way at the end of the week. All five of us knew straight away that, as far as we were concerned, his words were a formality. We knew also that ahead lay countless hours of hard work extending over months, years perhaps, and with outcomes none of us could anticipate and about which none of us was in the least concerned.

My companions are Hooper, a native Hong Konger; Mak, originally from Beijing; Krullo, from Indonesia and Nik, who was born in Thailand and moved to Hong Kong when he was a child. Hooper is the tallest – slender, loose-limbed, rangy. Mak is built on the lines of a Sumo wrestler, solid rather than fat, bear-like, more nimble than he looks. Krullo is compact, strongly muscled especially in the shoulders and arms. Nik is the shortest, and has powerful legs and remarkable agility. I'm not sure how I fit in. I am of medium build, I suppose I am versatile, with good co-ordination. I think I am good at being elusive.

We have two instructors, Wing and Chu. Both are in their late forties. Their heads are shaved. Wing is the taller, and is also a little thinner than Chu, who is stocky, with strong legs. Chu looks at you with round eyes and a fixed stare, like an owl, whereas Wing's glittering, restless gaze takes you in even as he also takes in what is going on around you. They are strong men, and you feel this partly because they don't display it.

***

So much comes back in an instant. We take a deep horse stance. Standing in front of us, Chu is like a tree, a 'great rooted blossomer' in perfect balance with the full strength and assurance of its nature. I have never seen a stance so deep. Chu's upper legs are parallel to the floor and so wide that they form a plane, entirely flat, horizontal to his body. His feet point straight forward and his lower legs are like springs, coiled but at ease in their tensile strength. The stance alone shows his authority. We follow him, and I see straight away that the standard among the five of us is high, and everyone knows this because the stance declares it. We hold for fifteen minutes. Not difficult. When we stand again in neutral, it is as if we have stepped together through a door into a different world.

***

We work until we are tired and then keep working and after that we practise skills until we can hardly think about what it is we are practising. Still, Chu warns against working too hard, because recovery is as important as the effort we put into the practice. Recovery is part of the work, he says, and we are to think of Lao Tzu's valley spirit – the mystery of the night that brings sleep and is as important as the day. Still, I want to keep pushing, keep working until I am burned right through, right out. It doesn't help that I am supposed to know better, and that it is important to avoid injuries. Once injured, the body is merciless because if you don't take time to heal, the injury becomes worse and then you are forced to take even more time. Nonetheless, twisted ankles, wrenched knees, strained backs, bruised hands, bloodied noses – these come and go. We all understand that it is better to avoid injuries, but also that injuries are unavoidable. And so we try not to be concerned but not to be reckless, working to the edge of what is endurable but not over the edge so that recovery is compromised. Sometimes it is hard to remember that exercise does not build muscle. Rather, it tears muscle down, and strength develops through rest. Just as Chu says.

***

The techniques are a vocabulary that increases until the number of new combinations becomes unpredictable – as with a child who learns a thousand words and can then put together an all but endless number of new sentences. Kung-Fu likewise teaches the body to speak. A beautiful piece of jade also speaks, so that you don't have to try to sell it, to force it on anyone. A buyer who doesn't hear the voice of what he's looking at, doesn't deserve to have it.

From the horse stance, a half-step back with the right leg and you are in a left-bow stance; with the left leg, a right bow. Each of these has an open and a closed side. The leading hand is always up, and forward with the front leg; the other hand is down, closer to the body, at the level of the navel. Both arms can close across the body to protect the open side, and the closed side is already defended. The key point about the six blocks is that you don't try to stop a strike; rather, from the bow stance, you protect the space around your body. If you learn to guard the space rather than chase the strike, you won't overreach. If you do overreach, you leave yourself open and your balance will be upset. Also, because the six blocks are economical and tight to the body, a block can quickly become a counter-strike. Of course, I had learned these basics before, but the main difference between pre-war practice and today is that today the significance of the techniques is explained in detail.

Wing leads the class. Chu watches and corrects us individually, without interrupting Wing's rhythm. This is demanding, because we have to focus on the proper performance of every repetition of every technique that Wing calls out, or else Chu will see the lapse and correct it.

***

I knew the Stance Form and *Kuen 1* from before the war, but not *Kuen 2*. Now, in learning *Kuen 2*, I realise that what Kai said is true: the forms are the heart of the system. Perhaps the Stance Form is an exception because it is a straightforward sequence of the main stances, linked together. But the *kuen* bring you into the soul itself of the Art, and they are complex, intricate. The elegant circular and linear motions, the fluidity and economy, strength and flexibility become a moving meditation that takes you out of yourself, so that the movements are no longer a combination of techniques but an energy that you embody, taking your mind and body into its own design, its own force field.

***

Slowly, the new knowledge brings us towards *Kuen 2* – outside forearm with inverted backhand, flexible hip with hidden distance, turning-stepping blocks, speed blocking, fallout technique, triangle stepping, four crescent kicks, six breakfalls, and elementary groundwork. Altogether, there are three *kuen* sequences, which eventually combine in a single unit, an extended form of great beauty and power. Deadly weapons can be made of jade; Kung-Fu can become a beautiful dance. Opposites converge.

***

Wing explains the three ranges – long, trapping, close. So far, almost all our training has been at long range. This is because the system that Sifu brings from his Shaolin roots is based on a series of ancient long-fist forms. I say 'based on' because, as with much else in the tradition, the originals are impossible to recover. The complexities of transmission and the contending claims made over centuries are hopelessly tangled and confused. Still, just as a language can preserve its identity despite the fact that there are many varieties of dialect and usage, so the long-fist forms give us a foundation that has a distinct identity despite the fact that it is interpreted in various ways. As the name implies, long-fist techniques are geared mainly to the distance at which high kicks and straight punches are most effective.

But at trapping range, the distance has closed, and we are almost toe to toe. Kicks have less importance and are kept low. The focus is on 'trapping' an opponent's arms, which is to say, neutralising his movements and swiftly turning close-in blocks into strikes. This is the special domain of Wing Chun, a main Shaolin style. Wing Chun requires less force and energy than the long-range techniques, and is said to be more 'internal'. Chu explains that we will learn more about Wing Chun at a later time. For now, we are to move directly from long range to close range, the third of the three main divisions. Close range is when you clinch with an opponent. You can deal with this while standing, or else take your opponent to the floor, the domain of groundwork. To those who are untrained in groundwork, says Wing, it is as if they are non-swimmers thrown into the deep end of a pool. And so it is better to be trained, even if all you do is learn to relax and float – because as long as you can float, you won't drown.

***

It is a shock to discover that years of practice – the hundreds of hours, countless thousands of repetitions – can be short-circuited in a flash by someone who just grabs hold of you and prevents you from striking. You are perhaps in a bear hug, a headlock, or you find yourself wrestling on the ground. To demonstrate, Chu grabbed me from behind. He is strong, and my arms were trapped. He lifted me up so that my feet were off the floor, then tipped me over and dumped me on the mat, pinning my arms and immobilising me with the weight of his body. "Try to get up!" It was Wing's voice, and I did what I could to move Chu off me. But the more I struggled, the tighter I seemed to be held. Soon I was squirming desperately, and Chu seemed to grow heavier by the moment until his weight felt enormous, and I found it hard to breathe. From some primitive source there came then a rush of what I suppose was adrenalin, a super-charge of energy laced with fear, and I heard myself making an inarticulate sound of panic as I drew on everything I had to get out of that anaconda grip. At last Chu relaxed and got up, bowing and shaking hands – a courtesy after every sparring and grappling session. I was wobbly and completely winded, and then I realised that in shaking hands, Chu was also supporting my elbow with his other hand to steady me, but without appearing to do so. The other students were watching, subdued.

"The first lesson is the hardest," said Wing, "and you have to keep learning it. The first lesson in a single word is 'conserve'. As you see, Philippe struggled and soon burned up his energy. When that happens, it is easy to panic, because the fear of being trapped, smothered, runs very deep – perhaps a memory of being born, the first life and death struggle. Also, all at once you find that your years of long-range practice come to nothing when the python wraps itself around you, and you are flat on your back and running out of air. It is a very bad feeling. But remember: every untrained opponent – which is to say, virtually any opponent who would confront you with violence, because only the untrained will bring violence to someone practised in the Art – believe me, every untrained person in Philippe's position will soon feel exhausted and helpless. Notice that Master Chu was relaxed the whole time. He used very little energy. 'Conserve': now you see what happens when you do, and what happens when you don't."

***

A day and a half later, and my body still vibrates in the aftermath of the adrenalin rush, the fight-or-flight hormone that gushed into the bloodstream at the very moment when fight and flight were both impossible. Could I have done better? The sheer force of the panic took me by surprise. It still does.

***

We begin with the standing techniques. What to do if your wrists are grabbed and how many ways they can be grabbed. How to deal with the bear hug, full nelson, choke-hold, headlock. In the standing position, there are three counters to the headlock and six more on the ground. We are leaving those six for later. The main thing is to know what to do, because then you can relax. In a bear hug, when you are grabbed from behind and your arms are trapped, the first counter-move is in turn to trap the opponent's hands with yours. He thought he had you in his grip, but now his hands are caught, and you are protecting yourself also from a possible choke-hold. Keep the clamp on his hands, and step either left or right into a deep horse stance. Your weight and the depth of the stance will make him bend over slightly, and it will be almost impossible for him to lift you. Because you have stepped left or right, a space will open along his centre line. Let us say that you step left. Then, to your right, his centre line is exposed, and your right hand delivers a knife-hand straight down and back, into his groin. He will certainly flinch backwards, allowing you to slide-step with your right leg into a diagonal horse, placing your right leg behind his left. Finally, a number four elbow strike is delivered by pivoting your body around your centre line, as the right elbow makes contact with his head and he spills back over your right leg. He either lets go under the weight of the strike, or holds on and falls with you to the ground, in which case your elbow drives down into his head or neck, with the weight of your body behind it. After that you will not likely have much further trouble, or, alternatively, you will easily acquire a controlling position on the ground.

So: the horse stance in two forms, a knife-hand and elbow strike combined with an understanding of how to preserve your centre line while destabilising his – all in a single sequence. As with a practised driver shifting gears, you learn to relax into the movements that you already know by heart and let the power-train take over.

***

We practise escaping and countering when grabbed or held in different ways. We will be at this for weeks, switching among ourselves to get the feel of the different body types. As always, repetition is the key. Wrist escapes until there is no more thinking about wrists or escaping, but only the interplay of the lines of force as the wrist-grab is thwarted and the opponent's energy turned back to its weak point at the thumb, so that it fails to hold. The same principles of containment, and then exploiting a weak point apply to virtually every attempt by an opponent to tackle and seize a person by bridging the gap from long to close range.

**

Another means of attack that bridges the gap – knives. Knives are dangerous, and the first line of defence is to run. Wing is emphatic about this. If you can't run, then find an object to put between yourself and the attacker: a chair, a shoe, a stick, pots, pans, candlesticks, a sweater wrapped around your arm. If nothing comes to hand, the Kung-Fu techniques are a last resort, and there are three main options. Again, each one combines a set of basic skills. In the first, a bell-block and retreat to the horse stance immobilises the arm holding the knife, which the defender lifts up and away as the horse stance moves back to an open-X and the bell-block hand delivers a backhand strike to the temple. The timing has to be precise, and the move should have the fluidity of a *kuen*, so that it unfolds in an escalating, and – for an opponent – unpredictable sequence that, once initiated, is virtually unstoppable by an untrained person. Similar principles apply to the other two main options. But there is also a good deal of improvisation in learning to defend against knife attacks. Bell-blocks, cross-blocks, cross-downward blocks, crescent kicks – all of these might be useful, and we drill over and over in improvised defence, all the while keeping an eye out for an opportunity to apply one of the standard sequences.

**

It is best to deal with a grabbing opponent standing up, but you might get tackled and taken down, or you might want to go to the ground anyway, in order to neutralise an overwhelming attack. Learning what to do on the ground requires a great amount of knowledge and practice, and at this stage we are to have only an introduction. Breakfalls come first – how to minimise the impact of being thrown, or falling. Then come the elementary throws. Wing says that we are to learn only the most practical and direct ways of taking an opponent to the floor. These involve front, side and rear grabs together with sweeps and leg-hooks, and an ability to use one's own falling body-weight to get the job done. We do this over and over. And then again. And again. Falling, grabbing, tripping, clinching, twisting, rolling. Falling, grabbing, tripping, clinching, twisting, rolling.

***

Today, Wing says that in the coming week we will spend the second part of the class in meditation. Further in the future, for some of us there will be a fuller engagement with meditation, and by 'fuller engagement' Wing means devoting several hours a day to the practice. Just as the groundwork takes us into a new arena, he says, so does meditation, which from now on will be a regular part of our training. We are to sit privately for short periods – twenty minutes or so – whenever we can. In the full scheme of things, meditation will be developed through Chi Gong exercises, mainly Bone Marrow Washing, which goes back to Ta Mo – though, again, the original Bone Marrow Washing form is lost. Meditation will not be a central part of our training now, but will be sufficient to remind us of how its yin aspect is the complementary opposite of the yang world of our long-fist system. Because we are young, yang is in the ascendant, our natural means of expression. But haven't we been learning to fall softly backwards in order to neutralise a powerful assailant by artfully taking him onto the ground? This also is yin-power, without which yang energy soon burns out. When you are burnt out, it is best to let yin replenish you. And so now we are learning to sit still.

Sometimes I catch a glimpse of how vast it all is – not so much a system to be learned as a way of life, a way of being in the world. As yang power declines with age, yin rises to balance it, but at the moment, I have no idea what it might mean to meditate for several hours each day, or what Bone Marrow Washing is. For now, meditation is, for me, mostly the moving meditation of the forms, the beauty of the skills, the rhythm of meeting, resisting, yielding, the preservation of the centre line in a tempest of activity. But I begin also to see the further pattern: from long-fist through the trapping-range skills to the close entanglements of grappling and then to the stillness of meditation.

***

Meditation can be done while sitting on a chair, in which case the hands are on the knees and the feet shoulder-width apart, and parallel. Or it can be done while lying on the right side, with the right hand under the right side of the face, pillowing the head, and the left hand lying along the left side, with knees slightly bent and feet together. It can also be done while standing, in which case the feet are slightly apart and the hands joined in front of the body. The best-known position is the lotus – either full or half. The meditator sits on the floor (or a cushion), with the legs folded underneath and the back straight. Hands are joined in the lap, and the fingers linked, with the thumb of the left hand meeting the middle finger of the same hand to form a circle, which in turn is interlinked with a similar circle made by the right hand, anchored on the ring finger of the left hand. The advantage of the lotus is that the strong, grounded triangle and straight back facilitate the upward flow of energy along the spine, though Wing says we are not to attend to that at present. At the introductory meeting, we were invited to take notes, and here are the main points, as close as I can get to Wing's words.

"When you sit, relax. Check your state of relaxation. Attend to your feet, knees, thighs, abdomen, hands, arms, chest, shoulders, neck, jaw. Make sure to relax your jaw and tongue – they will be tighter than you expect. Breathe quietly and easily. Let the breath come and go as it will, with no effort or strain. As you become conscious of your breath, rest the tip of your tongue on the roof of your mouth, just behind the upper front teeth. This is important – always do it when you meditate. The reasons will become clear when you have more knowledge. Make sure your back is straight, but do so without straining. Imagine a string running straight up from your spine – your centre line – through the top of your head, and align your neck and head with it. Check yourself again. Relax. Maintain good posture. Breathe easily, naturally. Now you are ready.

The exercise is simple. Focus your mind on your breath, and on your solar plexus, just under your breast bone, in the centre of your torso. As you inhale, empty your mind. As you exhale, focus your attention on your solar plexus area, and imagine the energy gathering there, then moving down to the area just below your navel. That area is called an elixir field, or *Tan Tien*. It is the first of three *Tan Tiens*. The second is at your solar plexus, and the third is at the crown of your head. For now, allow the breath to carry energy from the solar plexus to the lower *Tan Tien*. That is all. Don't attempt to do anything with the energy. Again, as you inhale, allow your mind to be empty. Exhale, feel the energy gathering in your solar plexus, and bring it down to the area below the navel, as instructed.

Random thoughts will float into your mind. Don't resist them. Just look past them, letting them drift away as you refocus on the out-breath. Also, you might have moments when your mind is not attending to your breath because it is, as it were, watching itself, aware of itself. But what I am calling 'itself', here, is not what you usually identify as 'you'. This is hard to explain, but you will know it when it happens. By and by, there is more say about this. For now, if such a thing happens, let it happen and don't disturb it – let the breath meditation go, and stay with that awareness the mind has of itself. And when it passes, let it go as well. Trying to force it to happen will prevent it from happening. So, return to the breath meditation. If you experience unusual physical sensations – for instance, if your stomach gurgles or you have small involuntary movements of your limbs – don't be concerned. But if for any reason you are concerned, come and see me. I don't want you to spend a lot of time in meditation. Twenty minutes or so a day is enough for our present purposes, and if you can't manage it every day, don't worry. We require very little. You are making the acquaintance, only, of something that you might get to know better when the time comes."

I practise my twenty minutes. It is not easy to be still. As Wing said, random thoughts pop up, and holding the mind steady is like balancing mercury on the back of a spoon. I had heard the expression 'monkey mind'. Now I understand. Patience. Don't go looking for a result. Don't fall asleep, because that is oblivion; don't follow the random thoughts, because that is distraction. Stay attentive between distraction and oblivion. The breathing exercise helps because it calms the mind. And, yes, the world seems calmer, quieter, more still, when I have finished.

***

The introduction of a new form marks a transition, and now we are learning *Kuen 3*. It ties into *Kuen 1* and *2*, to complete the sequence. As usual, we are taught individually, in the house. We learn as much as we can remember during the one-hour session. There is much repetition and we have a day, or sometimes two, between sessions to practise alone. After four or five sessions, the basic structure is in place. Then there are a couple of further sessions to refine the movements. Afterwards, we practise on our own for two weeks. Then there is another session, so that the performance can be assessed, and adjustments made. Hundreds of repetitions in the coming months bring us to the point where we don't think about the movements any more because the body dwells within what is expressed through the form itself. I do not know enough to describe the connection between meditation and the *kuen*, but I can feel it. In both, you let go of yourself. Anxieties, desires, hopes, fears, distractions, disappear. These are the conditioned habits, the huddled confinements of the prison-house of the ego with its resentments, petty hatreds, fears. The absence of ego-concern in the pure immediacy of the form is the Art in action, and there is no question here of winning and losing, victory and defeat, friend and foe. There is only the movement and the stillness at the centre of the movement. Combat, so-called, is merely the deflection of whatever would disrupt the beauty of the moving meditation and disturb the stillness at the centre. And so, the inner workings of meditation and the moving emptiness of the forms converge.

***

As Wing says, the hardest lesson in groundwork is the first lesson – 'conserve'. That is, don't waste energy, because, especially if you don't know what you are doing, you burn fuel more rapidly than you imagine possible. In turn, the key to conserving is to relax, and to exert yourself only to prevent a threatening move, such as a choke or an armbar. Otherwise, do whatever you can to encourage or provoke the opponent to keep working. For instance, make him grip more tightly by leaning your weight away from the place he is holding. And if he is trying to push you off, yield just enough so that he feels he is moving you, but at the same time anchor loosely onto a piece of his cloth – belt, collar, sleeve – so that he can't push you all the way off, even as he expends energy trying to do so. Don't lie flat on your back, but slightly on your side, curling up and into him. As he struggles for control, keep your arms inside his and fend outwards, which can be done without using a lot of effort. Anchor loosely at strategic points, securing your grip only when needed to keep him off balance or to keep him working. Use underhooks and overhooks, defensive and holding positions, shrimp-crawls and the guard position to stay safe. These manoeuvres keep you out of trouble, and within a couple of minutes an untrained opponent will start to build up an oxygen debt, and become worn out by his own efforts, so that it is easy for you then to take control.

With a trained opponent, you feel the difference immediately. A practised grappler knows how to conserve and he works to a purpose. Grappling then is a chess game, intricate in ways that an unpractised eye does not see. To the uninitiated, an expert display of groundwork can seem boring – as if nothing much is going on. In fact, every handgrip, foot-placement, minor shift of position is loaded with implication, purpose, craft. Frequently, a decisive move comes as if from nowhere – close-in, controlled, almost quiet. Achieving this level of expertise requires years of practice, and we are just beginning.

***

There is a basic groundwork form – overhooking, underhooking, posting out, reversing to maintain the defensive position. This sequence is practised with a partner until the moves become ingrained. Then we learn the five pins for control from top position. Each pin uses your body weight and a simple anchor. As an opponent struggles, you let your inertia do the work, focusing on staying anchored and holding your balance. If the opponent seems about to destabilise you, then you shift to one of the other pins, which can be applied from various positions around the opponent's body. So, as he shoves you in one direction in order to get free, he opens the door to a different pin. All that is necessary is to know what you are doing, and to know the five doors well enough to be able to step through them when they open, without expending energy. We practise the pins as a sequence: mount, side-mount, scarf, north-south, reverse-scarf. Again, to the untrained eye, the sequence might seem like a tangle of limbs, without design or purpose. But to a practised eye, the shifts and adjustments are according to plan – elegant, if you know how to look.

There is also a repertoire of finishing and escaping techniques. The five pins are an effective means of control, but, then, from each pin we are taught four finishing techniques. These are mainly armbars and locks, which can be applied so that you don't have to surrender the top position. This means that if you miss an opportunity, you can wait for another, or you can switch the pin and be on the lookout for one of the four finishes from there. We also have seventeen choke-holds, which, again, can be applied from any position. This repertoire of almost forty finishing options has to be learned by heart, so that you know, without reflecting, what is possible from any of the top positions.

If you happen to find yourself on the defensive, there are, likewise, four basic escape strategies for each pin used against you. These must be deployed patiently, and sometimes set up indirectly, because it is difficult to conserve energy while you are trying to escape. Consequently, if you find yourself pinned, the first strategy is not to struggle. Also, you must be careful not to give openings for a finishing move to be applied against you. If you find yourself on your back, with an opponent on top and in control, it is important to try to have your legs encircle his waist. You should also be anchored onto his upper body in order to bring it down, close to yours. Reversals can then be effected by knee turns, and chokes with the legs as well as with the hands and arms are possible. There are various techniques for escaping, and also for neutralising an opponent from this defensive position. As always, real knowledge of the entire repertoire of skills comes only from many hours of practice until, eventually, you find yourself grappling by feel, as well as by design.

***

We have been sparring quite a lot. As with groundwork, free-sparring is not for beginners, and requires a high level of mutual trust, as well as skill. Early in the training, one-step sparring is introduced as a way of practising the basic blocks, kicks, and strikes. In one-step sparring, a single striking technique is deployed at roughly twenty-five per cent of full speed, so that the appropriate block can be practised. The strikes should never make contact.

When a sufficient number of techniques has been learned, we move to contained sparring. This is the second of the three sparring levels, and involves continuous movement and the combining of techniques. Speed and power are held at less than forty per cent, and, again, strikes do not make contact. Students are in constant communication and can rerun sequences that might have exposed a defensive weakness, or were otherwise surprising or interesting. Contained sparring is excellent for learning, because you see and understand what is happening as you become familiar with the multiple combinations of techniques, both offensive and defensive.

The third level of sparring, free-sparring, was introduced to us in the weeks just before we began groundwork, at roughly the same time as we were practising the clinching positions and takedowns. In free-sparring there are no limits to speed and power, but no deliberate contact is made, except for the blocks. If a high kick or a punch gets through an opponent's defence, it must be pulled before it makes contact. Sometimes, mistakes are made and a blow lands. But these lapses are rare, and are accepted as accidents. Any indication of deliberately harmful intent would result in the student in question being immediately dismissed. A repeat accident by a student is scrutinised carefully, and steps are taken to ensure that further lapses do not occur.

One result of the long training period that precedes sparring is that an attitude of restraint and attentiveness gets built in as we come to understand, not just in our minds but also in our bodies, that Shaolin Chan Kung-Fu has nothing to do with competition in the usual coarse sense of trying to overwhelm an opponent. When the great masters of the northern and southern schools met to test their skills, they did so without landing blows. Their exchanges were an intricate dance, and in Chinese fantasy-versions of Kung-Fu the masters sometimes fly or levitate or spring lightly onto balconies or balance on the swaying branches of trees. None of this is meant literally. Rather, it represents the liberated spirit of the sparring exchange, the freeing of the ego in the play of movement: 'Who can tell the dancer from the dance'. Seen in this context, sparring is like performing a *kuen*. You are absorbed in the movement, vigilant but taken out of yourself, active but still. Meditation, *kuen*, sparring, are basically one and the same. The body suffers, yes – it is transient, it struggles to survive, and the ego clings to the body just as the body clings to the ego. "Don't hold onto life or fear death," says Chuang-Tzu. We are here until we will no longer be here, and while we are here we try to let the Tao shine. We need only to stop standing in our own light.

***

In free-sparring, every skill and technique comes into play. At first, there is a feeling of unpreparedness – of a great gulf between the years of patient learning, now confronted with the unpredictability of not knowing what an opponent will do. I remember it clearly. At first, the exchange seemed out of control. I felt that I had no technique whatsoever, and I was nervous. Then, because I was reacting anxiously, I became an easy target. Throughout, we are carefully observed by Chu and Wing, who comment only to remind us to acknowledge hits (strikes that get through our defences but were checked – as required – before contact was made).

Also, in free-sparring an opponent's unpredictability brings up something of the same adrenalin surge as groundwork does. Again, the deep hormonal activity of our survival instinct, governed by the amygdala deep in the brain, drives a primitive, blind anger and terror that can all too easily override technique, skill, calculation. But, through an increased exposure to sparring and grappling, the body learns to depend less on the adrenalin that fuels the urge to fight or flee. Instead, even in the midst of conflict we learn to remain calm, as the energy of the self-protective instincts is translated to the higher form of expression that we call the Art.

The match-ups among the five of us are interesting, and sometimes we also spar with Wing and Chu. I know very little about the personal lives of my training companions, or they about mine. We come here to work together, and when there is conversation we talk almost entirely about Kung-Fu. Yet, in another way, we know one another very well.

Sparring with Hooper: more difficult than I expected. He keeps out of reach because of his long limbs and light frame. He feints and strikes with surprising precision, and quickly pulls back and away. I can read his kicks easily because his long limbs mean that the arc is wide, and I have time to track it. But I need to be careful with his side-kick, especially as a counter when I try to move in. Bridging the gap to get inside Hooper's arms is the key to dealing with him effectively, but his bony elbows and forearms are quick to block, and he has good co-ordination. Also he comes back rapidly with strikes off the block. The most effective counter is to bring your own striking hand back very fast so that it, in turn, can block. Low roundhouse kicks to the knees and a simple, direct front snap kick work well against Hooper. But he is a handful, hard to get close to, and an accurate, fast striker who moves with elegance and control.

Mak is thickset and is a strong contrast to Hooper. The best strategy is to keep at a distance from Mak, and to move in and out quickly. He can throw powerful, low kicks, but not especially fast, so that he depends on a distracting upper-body attack to set up the low roundhouse. His blocks are strong, and at trapping range his strikes are hard and accurate. We have not yet learned many trapping-range techniques, but Mak is comfortable at that range, and also with grappling.

Krullo is athletic, and very strong. He is lithe and he has excellent timing and balance. He is deceptive because he seems to present openings that disappear as soon as you try to capitalise on them. He can slide away at the last moment and then return with force, taking advantage of the fact that you have committed yourself. He has an uncanny sense of where a training partner is off balance, and he can kick easily from any position, with excellent timing and an intuitive understanding of where an opponent's centre line is unstable.

Nik is agile, with a slight upper body and strong, short legs. Like many martial artists from Thailand, he is an excellent kicker. Because his legs are short, he can kick with lightning speed, even from surprisingly close range. Flexibility is also a big asset. In practice, he can stand on one leg while slowly raising his other knee, then extending the same leg straight up, while his body leans at a right angle to the floor. It is as if he does the splits vertically, while standing. And so, when you spar with Nik, even at close range he can deliver a side-kick straight up, between your hands. He is also expert at sole-sweeps, or hooking kicks executed close to the floor as you take a step towards him, so that the hook catches your foot just as it touches down. Sole-sweeps are difficult to anticipate, and they spill you in an eyeblink, hard onto the floor. For Nik, hands are mainly a distraction, opening the way to his kicks.

I am not sure how I fit in. Jack-of-all-trades, I suppose, without a dominant strength, but versatile. I think I have a not-bad sense of distance and timing. I block well and strike quickly, and my legs are good enough, but not great. I am elusive, hard to hit. But it is difficult to see one's self.

Our five different body-types and abilities mean that, as far as sparring is concerned, we get plenty of variety. And when Wing and Chu spar with us, things are different again. They are older and steadier, and one thing they have in common is that they are extremely difficult to get close to. They are always just out of reach, and they seem to put very little effort into making that happen. Also, they seem never to move fast. When they break down your defence and move in, they seem to be doing something obvious, unforced, never spectacular. Their blocks appear at the very last fraction of a second and are so close to the body that they can be converted rapidly into counter-strikes. The efficiency of their movements gives the appearance of being unhurried, and yet there is a sort of prestidigitation in the sheer simplicity of what they do as they move into the apparently obvious gaps and openings. We all know enough to understand how that kind of simplicity is anything but simple.

***

The warm-up exercises, basic stances and skills, strikes, kicks, forms and breakfalls, throws, groundwork, sparring, meditation – as if in a kaleidoscope, the hundreds of facets of what we have learned turn constantly into new patterns, at once recognisable and yet perpetually surprising. More time now than ever goes into personal practice, and, for all of us, the entire world is becoming, day by day, an extension of Kung-Fu.

As ever, Uncle is encouraging, and he asks me to do less and less for the business. He is busy. Sometimes he even seems a little impatient to get on and to leave me in Sifu's world.

BLOOD IN THE ALLEY

The foregoing selection of excerpts provides information about Philippe's Kung-Fu training between late 1946 and 1950. We do not learn much about the other aspects of his life, except for the fact that Uncle encouraged him to practise and to attend less to the jade business. But also, as we have seen, Uncle's apparent generosity was influenced by his desire to prevent Philippe from learning about the dubious Pak, not least because Uncle was increasingly falling victim to Pak's extortionist practices. He must have realised from the start that he was entering into a devil's bargain, but he probably thought that an increasingly effective post-war regulation of business as well as a less corrupt and more efficient police force, would help him to disengage. In addition, as I have suggested, he was holding some strategies of his own, in reserve.

To acquire better understanding of what happened on that fateful afternoon when everything changed for Philippe, I have consulted a wide variety of Hong Kong police and court records, as well as newspapers and magazines. But first, it is helpful to notice that an assortment of brief thoughts and impressions jotted down in the diaries suggest that Philippe did, of his own accord, come to feel that Uncle was behaving perhaps a little oddly, and was not quite himself.

'Uncle is fidgety. Working on his new deals. I practise. As usual, he leaves me be.'

'Uncle asked me to the store; then, at the last moment changed his mind.'

'Father is coming soon. Uncle needs cheering up – business these days can't be easy.'

'Uncle seemed more like himself. Father, always like himself.'

'I offered to work, but Uncle wouldn't hear of it. "Practice," he said. To be honest, a break from practice now and then would be welcome. But I can't say that.'

'Wonderful letter from Father. Very Victorian; also personable. Uncle is involved in international dealings, Father says. I had been wondering.'

'Uncle showed me some pieces from a new consignment. He wants a descriptive catalogue as soon as possible. They are splendid. "On the up and up," he says.'

Remarks such as these, though recorded briefly and in passing, do nonetheless suggest that from time to time Philippe felt some fugitive unease about Uncle, which might help to explain why Philippe acted so precipitously on the day to which our narrative now turns. Perhaps, even, a certain latent anxiety about Uncle was the touch paper for a highly combustible mixture of long-repressed feelings and unresolved tensions within Philippe himself.

Police records show that the event to which I refer occurred early on a Friday afternoon in May, 1950. Why Philippe showed up at the store unannounced is still not clear. Perhaps he had finished an assignment for Uncle – the catalogue, for example – and decided to deliver it. Perhaps he was curious about how things were going at the store – as we have seen, his work was confined to the warehouses, or to the correspondence and advertising to which he attended from home. Maybe his unease about Uncle extended further than the diary entries suggest, and he decided to investigate for himself. Anyhow, Philippe turned up unannounced on that day, at that time. In a journal, begun in Paris in the early summer of 1950, he describes what happened.

DIARY JULY, 1950

Writing requires you to imagine clearly, step by step, because you have to write, sentence by sentence. I recall going in by the back door, as usual – into the office behind the showroom. Then I heard the front door bang open, and voices arguing. Uncle's was one of them, and I saw that two men were standing close to him. They were taller and bigger, pressing in on him as they talked him down, loudly. They didn't hear me come in, and I waited, watching. One of the men had a large, heavy piece of fine jade in his hand, and there was a stack of banknotes on the counter. They were speaking Chinese, very quickly, but I was able to get the gist of it. Uncle was saying that they should not take the jade, and that the cash payment was enough – more, even – than was agreed. The men said that they had been instructed to take the jade, that very piece, and, if anything, the cash payment was not sufficient to cover the costs in question. Uncle then reached out to grab the jade, and one of the men shoved him forcefully into the wall. The other stepped forward and pushed him again. "We aren't here to hurt you," he said.

I stepped into the room. I remember how suddenly angry I was, and at the same time how utterly cold. The first man, the bigger of the two, set the jade on the counter, beside the money, and turned towards me. Both men were around forty years old, and both were strongly built. Thugs.

"Out!" I barked it rather than spoke it, and I remember that I was surprised by how strangely clear everything seemed. The first man, ignoring what I said, came towards me, his arms apart, hands held open in a conciliatory gesture as if to ask, 'And what might I be doing for you?' But as he stepped forward, I didn't hesitate.

The hidden distance came on its own. Hips pivot, shoulders turn on the centre line to add the width of the shoulders to the length of the striking arm, the fist vertical, aimed slightly upwards as the knees bend a little to thrust the power of the turned hips into the strike, which goes out fast but relaxed, like an iron ball on the end of a chain, directed not at the target but through it. For the first time, I delivered an actual, unrestrained Kung-Fu strike, and I felt the strangely gratifying crunch as his nose and upper teeth took the force of it, and the recoil as his head snapped back. He staggered, and lurched forward again, coming at me. Hidden distance is designed to keep space available, and a switch back to the bow position accompanied by a quick outside forearm block, took his lead hand away, and, as he turned to face me – his eyes already glazed – he tossed his head briefly to dispel the dizziness, leaving his throat unprotected from the panther fist that came in a straight line from the chambered hand. It is a dangerous blow, and when it struck I knew that I would have no more need to bother. The knuckles hit his windpipe so cleanly that I heard the snap as well as felt it, and he went down heavily, gargling and clutching his neck and face. I stomped hard on his head, landing my heel on his temple, and as he went unconscious, I saw his left leg twitching. His companion rushed wildly, furiously from behind him, but as he stepped over the twitching leg, his own front leg was exposed, and it was too easy to send a low roundhouse to his knee, collapsing his lead leg inwards. There is a lot of power in a roundhouse kick, and even though I threw it at little over half of full force, I could tell that his knee was damaged. He limped back a step – in retreat, I thought, but then I realised that he had reached inside his coat for a knife, and as I stepped forward to take advantage of his retreat, he slashed at my midriff. I hadn't seen the knife until it was too late, and I felt something like a bee sting in my abdomen as the slash caught me, though I suspected, even as it happened, that the cut was not deep. Still, I hesitated, and as I did, the knife-wielder lunged with a straight stab. The turn into a horse stance came, again, on its own, and so did the bell-block with the left arm, crashing into the wrist of his extended hand. My right arm was automatically raised as I stepped back into the horse, and it came down hard, grabbing his wrist where the bell-block had struck, almost precisely at the same time. I knew I had him then, and my anger was charged with a sense of elation and a pure, cold hatred, as my left hand swung his knife hand up and away, and I cross-stepped with the left leg to close the gap as a backhand strike with the right hand crashed into his temple. The striking hand then swept in a circle to come with an uppercut motion under his extended arm, beneath the elbow, as my left hand pushed his extended arm down at the moment of contact. The combined power of the sweeping uppercut, with the forearm crashing into the elbow joint as the other hand exerted a counter-force, instantly broke the elbow, so that the bone stuck out and the dislocated limb was crippled. As he fell back, I took the knife from his useless hand, and in a single blow, slashed him with it across the neck, not heavily, but enough to cause a flesh wound with a lot of bleeding. He was in shock – his knee and elbow were destroyed, and he was bleeding copiously. I felt the rush of a single, clear emotion – contempt – as I lifted the heavy jade ornament off the counter and smashed it onto his head. All this happened as if in an eyeblink. I had not even thought about what to do. Now both men were out cold on the floor, and I recall wishing that they would die.

Then I looked at Uncle. He was holding his head in his hands.

"Are you hurt?" I asked him. But when he looked up, I could see that he wasn't hurt; he was dismayed. For a moment, he didn't speak, but I could see that he was thinking hard. Then, he startled me by rushing to the back of the store and smashing the front of a glass cabinet with an onyx ashtray that had lain on the counter. He took out a handful of small, precious pieces.

"Here, take these," he said, "in your pocket, out of sight." Then he grabbed most of the money from the counter and stuffed it into my other pocket. "Go, immediately, but not home. Go to the Peacock Hotel, near Argyle Street and Canton Road. Take a room for three nights. Pay cash. Give a false name. Don't make contact with anyone. I will find you within three days, or I will send someone. You don't know what you have done. You shouldn't have come here – I have no idea why you came here. But now, go. There are three men outside – friends of these two. I will try to distract them. But I will have to pretend to set up an alarm, as if you are a robber caught in the act. They will follow you, and so you must go quickly. I am going to say that I never saw you before. That will fit with what these two know, and with the smash and grab that you have now committed. GO!" He pushed me out the back door, and, suddenly fearful, I ran.

I don't know how long a delay Uncle was able to effect, but I realised that the three men had caught a glimpse of me as I headed for a side street, perhaps a minute or two ahead of them. I didn't know my way about the Mid Levels, and I ran on instinct. I knew that I mustn't head for the Star Ferry terminal straight away. I would need to shake off the pursuers, and not run the risk of being cornered on the boat as I made my way to the hotel on Kowloon side. But they knew the area, and they tracked me, taking their time in order to catch me where they wanted. And so, when I turned into yet another alley, there they were. Two in front of me, and one, somehow, coming up behind.

Even now, it surprises me that I was calm. I would have to do my best to fight them off, despite the odds. When the first one rushed at me, I stopped him easily with a simple thrust kick aimed at his pelvis. He was jolted into a sort of V-shape, as his head and upper body shot forward and his legs stopped dead with the weight of the straight kick to his midriff, the mid-point of his balance. It seemed as if I had all the time in the world. A temple punch, thrust punch to the face, and a front snap kick to the groin came in rapid succession, probably in less than a second. As he crumpled and fell in front of me, I grabbed his hair and rammed his head hard onto the ground. But as number One went down, number Two had closed the gap and clinched with me. He had a knife, and I was lucky to have grabbed his wrist. But I was in trouble. He was stronger than I was, and he jammed me hard against a wall. I could barely move, and I was scarcely able to hang on to his wrist. With a side glance, I saw the third man coming rapidly to the assistance of the second, and I knew I had no chance. Yet, strangely – because you can't know these things until they happen – I didn't care. Then, incomprehensibly, Two started to struggle and all at once seemed to be gasping for air. I had no idea what was happening, until I saw that he was in a choke-hold from behind, supplied, apparently, by Three, who then twisted Two forcefully back, while grabbing the knife hand at the wrist, causing me to let it go. Three's choke-hold was weakened because he was using only his left arm, anchored onto his own shirt at the right shoulder, as his right hand held the knife up and away. Three then fell backwards, deliberately, hooking his legs around Two's thighs to immobilise him, while he forced the knife-hand closer to Two's body. Three then unhooked his right leg, and shrimp-crawled to his own left side, rolling Two quickly and smoothly onto his face, with the knife underneath. Surprisingly, I found myself admiring Three's technique, but I did not think about the knife, which in fact had gone into Two's chest, with the weight of his own and Three's body sending it in all the way. Three then stood up and rolled Two over, his heart's blood spurting from the wound. By this time, the first opponent was stirring. Three moved quickly, and with the same smooth power and precision, kicked One so squarely in the head that he was instantly senseless again. Then Three turned to face me.

It was Kai. "He would have killed you," he said, "and then me, if he had the chance, for trying to rescue you." I couldn't speak. Kai went on: "I have to stay here, and you have to go before this other one wakes up." As he said this, Kai looked around the alley, and quickly found what he wanted – a brick fallen loose from the wall. He picked it up, dipped it briefly in Two's blood and then said, "Get out of here. Do what your Uncle tells you." With that, he took a step back, and crashed his head violently against the wall. He staggered, and I could see blood running down the side of his face. He sat down, dazed, beside Two, and set the bloodied brick beside him.

"Run," he said, and I ran.

My whole world had changed, and I had no idea what was happening. But my first guess was that a Triad had Uncle in thrall. It was not difficult to see that. But what about Kai? And what about that horror in the alley? None of it made sense, and a man was dead. Instead of going to the Peacock Hotel, I found a small park on Kowloon side, and I sat on a bench, going over everything in my mind. I had not thought about the cut on my stomach, and now I saw that it had bled through my shirt. The wound wasn't serious, but I didn't try to pull the shirt away from the matted blood, in case it would bleed again.

Eventually, I decided to find the hotel. I had money, and Uncle had promised to make contact. I would check in, using a false name, as he said. But how would he find me, if he didn't know the name I was using? I decided to leave that to him, and so I made my way to the Peacock, where I got a single room, and waited.

The same evening, Uncle turned up. He had someone with him – a late-middle-aged man who might have been Thai or Cambodian, and who turned out to be a doctor and also a personal friend.

"First, the cut," Uncle said. "I saw what happened."

Without a word, the doctor examined the wound as I lay on the bed. He cleaned it, dressed it, and gave me penicillin as a precaution.

"Not much. Flesh only," he said. "Lucky."

He chatted briefly with Uncle, but I could not hear what they said. Then the doctor left. Uncle was cool and impersonal, and I knew that he was angry.

"You have to leave Hong Kong. I will send your passport, and money. We will get you out by boat to Shanghai, and then you fly to Paris. Your father is there, and will meet you."

I had questions, but Uncle clearly did not want to hear them. He would tell me, he said, as much as I needed to know. The afternoon's events were very serious, and the police were searching for me. One man is dead in an alley, and two others are injured. At the store, two men are injured, one seriously. None of this should have happened. The men at the store would not have harmed me. Besides, I shouldn't have been there in the first place. He paused to let that sink in.

"As no doubt you guessed, at the store you were witness to extortion. How I got involved doesn't matter. All I can tell you is that I have been working for some time on a plan to turn the tables on those people. Things had almost come to a head – and now this."

"Kai?" I said.

"In a moment. First, nobody connected to that gang knows who you are. I took care not to expose you to any of that so you could not become a hostage to those thugs. I have reported that you broke into the store and were plundering it when we interrupted you. You then fled with some money and several valuable pieces of jade. You are a thief, caught in the act. When you fled, you were pursued and you killed a man and disabled two others, striking one of them with a brick. And so you are quite the fearsome fellow. But now you must disappear. As it happens, this will not be difficult. None of the men knows you, and there is so much robbery in Hong Kong that the police will assume that you are one of a thousand thieves on their list. Also, the police know full well that the men in the alley are violent criminals, and will be glad enough to get rid of them, though they can't drop the case without appearing to look further into it. They will get nowhere, and then they will drop it. I should tell you – in absolute confidence – that Kai was planted years ago inside that gang. He is what the Triads call a '25' – that is, a spy, an informer. He has been gathering documents and other information and we are now on the edge of exposing Pak for what he is. We must have hard evidence that not even the corrupt police can ignore or suppress. We will bring this evidence to the newspapers, mainly to ensure that the police don't try to evade the issue. As you can guess, Kai is in jeopardy. But his quick thinking saved your life in the alley, and probably his own. The Triad does not suspect him, because he was found unconscious, with a head wound. The one man who could have identified him would have killed you without hesitation, but he himself now is dead. Perhaps the plan to expose Pak – the Triad boss – will hold, but in another way it is already a disaster. Violence and death are the stock and trade of Pak's world, not ours, but now we have joined him in this madness."

Uncle paused, and I realised how completely I had failed. The standards of Kung-Fu that I thought had become as important to me as breathing itself, now ranged themselves against me. My heart sank. I said nothing.

"You will be picked up in the morning. Remember, no one has any cause to suspect you, and there are ways and means to pre-date your departure, if need be. So I am not concerned. As I said, your father will meet you in Paris. I will send some business to you there, but you will need to get a job and to fend for yourself for a while. Your Kung-Fu training will have to stop, of course. But when the time is right, perhaps a teacher will appear and you can continue, if you wish. Now I have to go. Be ready at 6:00 a.m. Clothes and supplies will be brought to you in the morning. The owner here owes me a favour – you might have guessed. So, good luck. Rest this evening. Use the hotel as you like, and charge everything to the room."

He made a little bow and stepped backwards, taking his leave.

I could feel his disapproval, his coolness, and I realised what a disaster I had created. Still, I have to admit, I couldn't help feeling some secret pleasure, in doing damage to those scum at the store.

EMIGRÉ

And so Philippe went to Paris. His father was working there, and with his assistance, Philippe rented a small apartment in the cinquième. By and by, he found a job in a bookstore, where he specialised in rare Chinese and Asian editions. But the shock of what happened in Hong Kong, once it had sunk in, exhausted him and undermined his confidence, so that he did not look for work until several weeks after his arrival. Later, he would write that the two years he spent in Paris were the worst period of his life. He was depressed, lonely, unable to make sense of the disruption of his life. His distress is clear in the diaries that he began shortly after his arrival, as he struggled to deal with his new situation.

DIARY MAY-JUNE, 1950

For the moment I am OK – enough books, money. I walk to Notre Dame, to be cradled in the silence, to become anonymous in that ancient forest-grove of stone. Our Lady assented to the sword in her heart – which her son says is better than putting a sword into someone else's.

***

Wet streets, little cafés, awnings soaked and dripping, outside tables empty, yellow lights, cigarette smoke, a glint of glasses, hands catching the rhythms of conversation, terrines, small white coffee cups, a quiet hubbub. I look in. The rain is coming through my clothes – a quick chill as it touches down.

***

Father is not in Paris permanently, and asks if I would prefer London. I tell him, no, Paris is fine. I don't mind being by myself. Father is delicate about the Hong Kong debacle. Vaguely, he expresses sorrow for 'the circumstances' and then assures me that Paris is making excellent headway after the war. There are good opportunities, and he could make suggestions. I appreciate his concern. I am careful not to be churlish and I fake a little optimism.

***

I drink more than I should, but too much is sometimes consoling. Why not – immoderation at moderate intervals.

***

Today, Father left. He must suffer too, but I don't know. I tell him that I will look for a job. He knows that Uncle is sending business for me and has opened a bank account in my name so that I can receive funds, if necessary. I know that Father knows the story, but he doesn't want to go into it. I decide that this is diplomatic caution. What he hasn't heard he can deny hearing without perjuring himself, should it come to that. But it turns my stomach now to think of doing whatever work Uncle has in mind. I don't want to think about it at all.

***

The Louvre – impressive to the point of indecency, and yet Delacroix's great picture of revolution – what a thing. The dead and wounded, the people hauled out at night and shot, form the base of a pyramid, its foundation. At the apex, the determined stride of the bare-breasted woman, front and centre, punching the air, fuelling the storm around her. She has grubby feet, an offence to pictorial propriety. She is soiled and not beautiful, a defiance of convention. She is a woman of the streets and the ancient Roman Libertas, on the rampage until the last king lies strangled in the entrails of the last priest, the revenge of violence against violation, of terror against tyranny. What would Lao Tzu say?

***

I walk at night, sleep late. In Montmartre, the girls pace up and down, vivid for a moment under their territorial streetlights. A glimpse, then back into the shadows, but available if you walk into the half-light between streetlight and doorway, streetlight and alleyway, and agree on a price. I slouch past and they never try to catch my eye, never beckon. They know that nothing stirs in me. I want only the late-night streets potent with emptiness, silent except for a few walkers drifting, spectral. I tell myself that the night is not entirely dark, the streets not entirely empty, that there is some contentment in the absence of desire.

***

The city gets into you, the clutter and bric-a-brac of the cinquième, the absurd, splendid gesture of the Champs Elysée, the confidence of the grand boulevards and the intimate elegance of the little ones, the river dividing it all yet holding it all together, the magical island its beating heart, the clamour of the markets feeding the menagerie of the city's appetites.

***

I make applications, so that I can feel I am doing something. And I read: Dostoevsky, Shakespeare, Freud, Dumas, Balzac. How well the great ones know the intimate betrayals and self-betrayals that we think of as our best intentions, our virtues. How does Macbeth's courage become a nightmare? Don't those witches haunt us all?

***

A bookstore in Boulevard St Germain takes the plunge, and I am to work in Chinese antiquities. By coincidence, a package arrived from Uncle. My heart sank. But then, a surprise. It contained a list of desiderata – items to look for, possibly to purchase. But there were no instructions, no appointments, no expectations. Uncle has also deposited money in my account, for expenses. I guess he wants to have a back-up – in case he might need it – to explain my leaving Hong Kong. A touch of the old horror comes back. Where is Kai? What about Pak? What about Uncle?

***

Being able to read and speak Chinese is my main asset, though my English also adds value. Basically, I am overqualified and they know it. I tell them I have come from Montreal to improve my French. It is easy for them to accept this, because for them Parisian French is the only French. Nothing succeeds like flattery when it condones a prejudice.

The work has points of interest, but mostly it is boring. I am an exotic because I speak French with a strange accent and I can rattle on in Chinese. I am supposed to work on bibliographies, cataloguing, ordering, but the management uses me also to deal directly with customers. Without being told, I know that they want me to put on a show to help to boost the sale of some rare edition, to explain illustrations, or the calligraphic wall-hangings in which the store also deals. The great Dutch painter, Vincent van Gogh, once worked in an art dealership and got fired because he told customers what he really thought of the paintings they were considering. He did his best to talk them out of buying things that he himself didn't like, and the management soon ran him out the door. For me – the management's darling – it is the reverse. I do exactly what they want.

***

Father is here for two weeks, then off to Geneva. I tell him about my job. He is pleased – or as pleased as it is possible for him to be. He wants to know details and he listens well. I realise I am gabbling, and how quietly expert he is in letting me talk. The wine helps. He hardly drinks anything, but he is not an abstainer. I ask how things are going in Hong Kong, and he says all is well, no need to worry. I don't come right out and say what is on my mind because I don't know how much he knows, but I find myself muttering, "You know about it. The trouble." Contrary to the habit of the good listener, he stops me gently, firmly.

"But no longer. There is no trouble now. Uncle sends good wishes. He hopes you are keeping your eye open for the jade, as he asked."

"I'm working on the jade," I say. "The job helps. I have interesting leads." He smiles slightly, making the briefest bowing movement with his head.

"Good," he says. We talk more, and we both know that we are ignoring the elephant in the room. And so I keep my bad conscience to myself, and he, as usual, stays carefully poised on the safe side.

**

The Russian girl who came into the store to look at the Chinese wall-hanging in the window – clearly, she wasn't going to buy it. But she had it taken down anyway. She was a raggedy creature, carelessly dressed though with flair, a patchwork of colours, not fashionable but with style. She had a shock of wild, wiry, blondish hair. It was as if she walked around in a perpetually charged field of static electricity that might give off sparks on contact. She introduced herself in English to the salesman, Guillaume, and I was fetched to explain the calligraphy. She said that she was Russian, not all that bad at French but better at English. I suspect that Guillaume wanted to leave it to me to move her on.

"It's eighteenth century," I tell her. "Quite rare. Cursive script, sometimes called 'grass script', very beautiful, as you see, with three abstract shapes that are difficult to read. It's a version of a standard poem, though of course the poem is remade because of how the calligrapher interprets it. A perfect bond between the literary and the painterly."

She said she knew about the literary and painterly. There was a good deal of interest in that sort of thing in the experimental poetry scene in San Francisco, which is why, actually, she wanted to take a look. Did I know about that, in San Francisco? I didn't. Perhaps I'd been talking down to her, and now she was setting things right.

"Go to San Francisco," she said. "It's liberating." Her tone was cheerful, spiced with mockery, and she tossed the words over her shoulder as she took her leave.

**

115

Her name is Alyona – Anya to her friends. If we could see our place in the immense interweave of our comings and goings, the interminable sentence of our beginnings and endings across the aeons of time, wouldn't we know in such a meeting that we are here again, and isn't every meeting a reunion? The words still ring clear, teasing.

"Hey, Mister Calligraphy." She is sitting at a café in the Boulevard St Germain, not far from the store. "I'll buy you a coffee if you take me to San Francisco."

"Of course," I say. And so we meet and talk, talk and meet. She laughs, amused, keeping just out of reach – mocking, enchanting.

The Paris journal ends here, with Philippe meeting Anya. He fell for her, of course, and during the next eighteen months they developed an intense, intimate relationship. As far as I can tell, it was, for him, the first of its kind. I have tried to locate Anya, but without success. After she went back to Russia, she seems to have disappeared from Philippe's life. The small number of leads that I managed to turn up indicate that she is still there, but I have been unable to make contact.

While she was in England, shortly before she returned to Russia, Anya and Philippe wrote to one another, and Philippe also made notes and jottings about her. These are often impressionistic, and sometimes they are a preparation for his letters. From these assorted materials, a picture emerges.

Anya had saved money and was travelling, but, after she met Philippe, she decided to stay with him, in Paris. When their paths first crossed, she was twenty-five years old. Her parents were divorced. Her mother, who was English, had remarried and lived in London, where she worked in a bank. Her father, who was Russian, lived in Moscow. Anya began her schooling in Russia, while her parents were still together and were living there. When they separated and her mother moved back to England in 1930, Anya went with her. She was an unruly child, and by age eight she was placed in a boarding school. Eventually, the school couldn't handle her, and in 1938 she was packed off, at her own request, to Russia, and then to a school in Belgium, where she seemed to do well until, at age fifteen, she seduced a teacher. The scandal was covered up, and Anya returned once more to England. Her schooling continued with private tutors, as well as more than one frustrated counsellor, in preparation for her matriculation exams. She was clever, and she gained admission to a university in the south of England. During the war, she and her mother had moved out of London and were living with relatives in a small town near Southampton. Attending university at first appealed to Anya, because it meant independence. But the times were troubled – as she was herself – and she didn't last beyond the first year. After that, she worked at an assortment of jobs. How she managed to convince a broad range of people to hire her is unclear, but she could be charming, vibrant, seductive, and she was intelligent and effortlessly versatile. She had plenty of admirers, including ex-lovers who could be called upon, no doubt, for hyperbolic references. And she was good at making up stories. There are a few black and white photos of her among Philippe's papers. She had a shock of blonde hair, parted in the middle and flying out like wings on either side – a great, bristling fan, startling, wild. She is, what the French call *belle laide* – beautiful and unbeautiful at the same time, not pretty yet arresting, unconventional but captivating because of a natural piquancy and vividness that gave even her imperfections a captivating, personal energy. In a few photos she smiles like some mischievous fairy, innocent but with a glimmer of ancient knowingness that leads you on but also warns you off; a primitive amoral power of attraction. She had worked at all sorts of jobs – waitress, editor, language teacher, small art gallery manager, kindergarten assistant, barmaid, museum guide. There must be others that I don't know about. She seems to have changed jobs much as she changed moods, and in her personal life she vacillated often between electrically charged enthusiasm and crushing disappointment. She could switch unpredictably from uninhibited affection to fierce hostility. She was a force of nature such as Philippe had never encountered, and from the start he knew he was in over his head. Yet Philippe had his own magnetism, and he also was far from run-of-the-mill. Understandably, Anya fell for him, as he for her. And yet it is also understandable that their relationship was unlikely to last. Philippe's ghosts – the anger, the sense of abandonment that had shaped his life from his early years, together with the events in Hong Kong that he would have to keep from her – could not stay well enough hidden from the white heat of Anya's chaotic intensities and her ruthless power of insight. Nor could he endure to disclose those vulnerabilities to her. The very thought terrified him.

The break-up occurred approximately a year and a half after the first meeting in the bookstore. Throughout their relationship, Anya had gone to London for short visits to her mother, and she sent cards and letters. On the last of these visits, she wrote to say that her father was ill in Moscow, and she was going to see him. En route, she sent Philippe a letter. As far as I can tell, that was the last time he heard from her:

> We know we have not been happy these past months. I am sorry. They are better than us, those normal people. We are the damaged ones. But do not worry, my sweet Pip, because what you have loved well will not be lost to you. We have loved well and so we will not ever lose one another. I am very sorry for the harm I have caused. Goodbye, and love forever. Alyona.

The details of what happened between them that caused them not to be doing well are unclear, but fact remains that the aftermath of the break-up was the most difficult period of Philippe's adult life – his dark night of the soul – and during this time he wrote the wintry garden passage I cited earlier, containing the bleak conclusion that 'love kills everything'.

Thanks to Anya's gregariousness, she and Philippe had numerous friends in Paris, from whom Philippe now found support. Whether through their encouragement or by his own inclination (he was an avid reader of Freud), he sought professional help. There is good evidence for this because approximately six months after the break-up, he began a journal. It takes the form of a dialogue, and it draws, clearly, on his psychotherapeutic experience. And so, to fill out this period of his life, I will let the journal speak for itself, though I omit materials that seem to me to be too personal to be included here.

DIARY JULY, 1952

The weeks pass. There is not much sense of time. It is as if the thread of myself is suspended in a dense, heavy fluid, pressing, formless. I dream that if I keep steady the thread will gather crystals – something will take shape – but the slightest agitation and everything dissolves again. Be still, still. And yet I twist instead inside the dark volume and nothing comes, no shape, no form, days at a time. Perhaps, then, a single crystal, a tiny asterisk – but at once every facet of it reflects some detail I remember about you, and I am lost again in confusion.

A great theologian writes that we can only truly love those who have hurt us. I try to believe this. I try to understand because we can never truly understand what we do not love. I have helpers. Friends who listen, professional listeners, sometimes strangers who don't know anything about me but who listen and tell me things. I give them all a single name: Hermes.

"You are in mourning," Hermes says. "Yes," I tell him, "I can't find words. There is only the grief, and when I open my mouth to speak, there is no sound. I am destroyed, entirely, and I can't say why. What happened was – impossible."

Hermes: Why impossible?

Self: Because of what we had together, what we knew together. She liked to cite the medieval story of Tristan and Iseult: 'For she was he and he was she'. She wrote out a favourite passage, and could cite it by heart: 'But I will ask one thing: to whichever corners of the earth you go, take care of yourself, my life. For when I am orphaned of you, then I, your life, will have perished. I will guard myself, your life, with jealous care, not for my sake, but yours, knowing that your life is one with mine'. I believed it. I cannot not believe it.

Hermes: Medieval romance. The world has passed on. She also has passed on. Still believing, perhaps?

Self: She has to believe. Otherwise there is no sense.

Hermes: She was a difficult child, a troubled teenager. You say that, early in her life, she deliberately hurt herself – cutting, self-starvation. Later, she was promiscuous. When you got close to her, you found a powerful adulation – dependency, even – and a great intensity of feeling. But then you also encountered fits of overpowering anger and disappointment.

Self: What does this explain?

Hermes: There is a name for it – which means, at least, that you are not alone. It is a disorder that is difficult to classify and even more difficult to manage. But what really concerns us now is your involvement, and what it shows you. You might not be flattered. Her trouble started in childhood, with the earliest bonding process. Infants begin to form a sense of self when they are able to internalise separation from the mother. Once an infant knows and can trust that the mother will come back – when the infant is left for a while, for instance – then rage and anxiety are contained, and this containment is the seedbed that nurtures the provisional unity we call the self. If, for whatever reason – and there are many – the bonding and separation process doesn't occur, there is no such containedness, no viable sense of self, and, instead, a powerful, generalised anxiety, as well as deep feelings of unworthiness and a terrible insecurity punctuated by outbursts of anger. The main thing is that such people are highly dependent on relationships because they see in others the values that they think will sustain them as well. So, they idealise, and live through some other person, who is imagined, as it were, as having got it all together. But there is always disappointment. The demands are too intense, angst-driven, and the admired person can never give enough, cannot fill the void. Typically, such people move on, often impetuously, and don't look back, or think of themselves as responsible. It's the other who's to blame for not living up to the ideal. Yet, such people can also be wonderfully affectionate. Because the normal boundaries of the self are not in place, they are capable of thrilling, emotional intensity, or surprising, unguarded openness. For instance, they might act as if they are a longtime friend even to a complete stranger – someone encountered in a line-up at a checkout, or on a bus, in a café. And the whole thing starts over.

I see you recognise something. So I'll go on to you. As you might see, she took your values to heart, mirrored your desires. You experienced this as a wonderful reciprocation – 'for she was he and he was she'. And so you saw yourself mirrored in her, and you believed that what you saw was actually *her*. Then, when she did the impossible and left, it was just that, impossible. No one believing what you believed could have done it. But what you saw was yourself reflected, as a role she was trying on. Inevitably, you were disappointing because you were less than the perfection she admired, and the empty place at the centre would need another idealised person who, eventually, will not live up to the task either. She showed you your own face in the glass of herself, and then she smashed the glass and your world disintegrated.

Self: So, love seeks understanding and this is what it gets – narcissistic delusion. But isn't she more complex than just a list of behavioural patterns? Isn't she more human, more this person, whom you do not know?

Hermes: Yes. The mystery endures, of course. She is indeed a person, irreducibly complex, unique, and I cannot say what you know of her as such. Still, the fact remains that what troubles her can be described in general terms. Think of it this way: every patient in a hospital is unique, but usually an accurate diagnosis of their illnesses can be made. Appendicitis, pneumonia, are conditions that afflict people who in themselves remain utterly individual. In this way, what I have described to you is a recognisable pattern of behaviour, shared by others.

Self: I am afraid of being locked into patterns. What about her, herself – her own suffering?

Hermes: You can do nothing about her suffering. But you also are a wounded soldier, so think of that.

Self: I have destructive tendencies, yes, I'm sure. Now I suppose you are going to tell me about them.

Hermes: Well, then let us turn the mirror around. Tell me about your parents – your mother, for instance.

Self: My mother? She died when I was twelve. I remember not wanting to live. I remember being filled with anger, beyond even the grief that I could not properly feel but that was suffocating me nonetheless. I remember imagining that she was not really dead, and I would find her. I told myself that she was away on a trip, and my father, who travelled a lot, was looking for her. She would come back.

Hermes: Your father?

Self: He is a diplomat. He travels. He is clever and aloof. He is also generous and good, even though he is not exactly warm. He was not often around when I was young. Indeed, I have no idea how he dealt with my mother's death, how he felt about it.

Hermes: So, you have fended off the world, even as you have fought to grow up in it. You mentioned going in for martial arts. I assume you found structure there, authority you could depend on, a means of expressing your anger without doing damage – if I understand correctly. Why did you stop?

Self: It is a long story. I failed. I can't do it any more.

Hermes: Anger got the upper hand, am I right? And so you gravitated to a damaged woman – a woman whom you might save, who idealised you, who flattered you and bolstered your self-worth, even as she sought to shape herself according to the image she had of you. The intensity of that mutual deception must have been as ecstatic as it was disastrous. It is as if two hands, palms together, fingers interlaced, are locked and gripping hard out of fear of letting go. But those hands are better employed by remaining open, side by side, facing the world, with work to do, together. And all the while, you were struggling to grow up, but you never did. The values that shape you – a mix of medieval Catholicism, Eastern monastic asceticism, modern critical intelligence – these are the means that you latched onto to contain your own trauma. As such, they are products of necessity, not freedom.

Self: But what am I supposed to do if everything I choose is blindly shaped by childhood anxieties and absences?

Hermes: Your values can, in themselves, be admirable. The point is whether or not they can, or should, survive the elimination of the childish needs, the emotional distress that required them to be constructed in the first place. Can what you believe be resurrected after your journey, your dark night – resurrected in a free form because of how belief now is brought to consciousness, understood, chosen again. This is the only freedom – freedom from the iron routines of necessity – and this freedom grows through the process of re-evaluation, renewed understanding, so that what you once needed to protect you, you can now choose freely, if there continues to be a value for you in doing so.

Self: But how is it that the suffering doesn't go away? Even when I understand it?

Hermes: It is the nature of the wound that it never heals. You are a man trying to make his way, and for that you must be wounded.

Otherwise you never become a man, but, instead, another of the grown-up children we see all around us, creating havoc out of their infantile fears and confusions.

In the following months, Philippe worked at the kind of re-evaluation he had written about, as he attempted to put his life in order. His emotional struggles during this period are unrecorded, but he continued to work at the bookstore, and to meet with friends. He also began to make plans for the future. These included a resolve to begin again with Kung-Fu, if he could. I do not know if he discussed the matter with his father first, but it is clear that Philippe and Uncle were in contact in 1953. Among the diaries is a collection of Hong Kong newspaper cuttings from 1952, in an envelope date-stamped Hong Kong, March, 1953. These cuttings deal with the arrest, trial and conviction of Pak as well as several of his associates who were likewise charged with extortion, tax evasion, and racketeering. Uncle was a key witness, but his was not the only business targeted by Pak and by other, loosely associated Triads within the same criminal network. The reports say that incriminating documents were gathered during the previous years by undercover police, with the co-operation of business leaders who were victims of organised crime. Gang warfare had also contributed to Pak's demise. A number of known criminals had been killed, apparently because of divisions within their own ranks, or by other gangs. Because of lack of evidence, no charges had been laid, but the police were confident that order had been restored. Pak's property and assets had been seized, pending judicial proceedings whereby aggrieved business owners were suing for compensation.

 Philippe probably received this bundle of cuttings just before he wrote to Uncle to ask about resuming Kung-Fu. Then, in January, 1954, he received a reply, written in Chinese. It contains the following paragraph, which I cite here in translation: 'Kung-Fu for the future is possible. In Hong Kong it is not possible. Sifu agrees you should try and sends good luck. Whatever we find, I will let you know.' Philippe had made the first move, and, in response, Uncle and Sifu were at least tentatively co-operative. The newspaper clippings would have been sent to communicate to Philippe that the troubles in Hong Kong were largely resolved, while also giving him some sense of the larger course of events there. Still, as Uncle's letter makes clear, neither he nor Sifu was keen for Philippe to return.

Then, in July, 1954, Philippe received another letter, informing him that if he were serious about resuming Kung-Fu, arrangements could be made, but he would have to move to the United States, perhaps for an extended period of time. There is no record of how Philippe felt about this, but I have pieced together what seems to be a likely story.

First, Philippe's backers in Hong Kong were willing to give him a chance, and their reasons would become clearer to Philippe at a later date. Probably, in light of the criminal violence and sensational events of the recent past, it would be prudent to keep him away from Hong Kong. Also, it seems likely that neither Uncle nor Sifu was convinced that Philippe would succeed if he did return to training. If he failed, it would be better for all concerned if that happened somewhere else than in Hong Kong. Third, Philippe was going to have to prove his resolve, and it wouldn't help to make things too easy. And so, the first test was to require that Philippe leave his job in Paris and move to the United States. Uncle explained that he had a business deal about to get under way there, in one of the main east coast cities (I have been asked not to be more specific), and Philippe could help with negotiations. The salary would pay for his travel expenses, and there would be a little over. When the business was concluded, Philippe would have a meeting with some Shaolin Chan representatives, and would receive instructions. Although, as ever, there would be no pressure, it would help everybody concerned if Philippe were to make a serious commitment before uprooting himself from Paris.

Uncle's business deal was probably an ad hoc arrangement to facilitate Philippe's move, but the relocation to America is in itself a matter of some interest. As we have seen, many Kung-Fu masters who fled from China, beginning in the 1930s, went to the United States, and by the 1950s there were well-organised Kung-Fu groups in several major cities. Also, there were close contacts between many of these groups and Hong Kong. Clearly, the organisers of one such group agreed to oversee Philippe's progress. To do this, they intended to send him to one of the retreat centres that exist in a small number of locations on the east and west coasts, and which selected students visit for periods of intensive training. I have visited the centre chosen for Philippe, though I cannot give details about its location. It consists of a converted farmhouse, which, together with the outbuildings, can accommodate up to twenty students. Eventually, Philippe found his way there, and because he now had more time and more incentive to write, he began again with his diaries. Although the record of his training is intermittent, the following excerpts provide a sufficiently clear account of his story, in his own words.

THE FARM

DIARY AUGUST, 1954 – JANUARY, 1955

Three hours by bus, and an hour's walk. There must be an easier way. Still, it was good to arrive and to know I was expected.

The main building is more like a manse than a farmhouse. It stands on a low hill overlooking a broad stretch of fields interspersed with stands of trees, framed by further hills in the distance. A restful, scalloped undulation of greens and browns, bright wet grass, a clear, eggshell sky – so the turning year declares the beauty of the change it heralds.

Fifty yards or so down from the main house is a large enclosed yard with three converted farm buildings. These serve as a dormitory, a kitchen, and a training hall. There are showers, toilets, and facilities for washing clothes. When I arrived, the whole place seemed deserted, as in fact it was, except for James.

Like myself, James is half-Chinese, half-Caucasian. Unlike myself, he is entirely American, born in Philadelphia, raised in New York. I guess that he is in his mid-to-late twenties. As with many people I have met in the Kung-Fu world, he is open and friendly, relaxed, with an athletic poise and a courteous demeanour that invites reciprocation. He explains that he will be my teacher. "Good," I say, "I look forward." He is quite a bit younger than I am, but I tell myself that doesn't matter. He explains that I am scheduled to be here for six months, and I will stay in the dormitory. Other students are due to arrive soon. He isn't sure how many – six, perhaps ten. Each group stays for a month, and the students are, mostly, young people from the city. They have their own lives, jobs, responsibilities, but they have all received Kung-Fu training beyond the basics. Normally, they train in small schools, and, at intervals, a selected number are invited to come here for an intensive review to co-ordinate and develop their knowledge. And so the traditions are kept alive, James says, even while we adapt them to changing times and circumstances. He goes on to explain that three, perhaps four, groups will come during my six-month stay, and I will train with them. In the early evening, when the students have free time, James and I are to train together for an extra hour. Also, there are chores around the farm, and the students, myself included, will help with those.

I ask about my status, how I fit in. James says that I will simply be a member of the class. For the most part, the students don't know one another, and so I will fit in, and no explanation is required. I have questions, but he sees them coming and heads them off. "I am here to train you," he says, "as long as you want. Come – let's look around."

He turns, and I follow as he shows me the kitchen, eating area, dormitory, showers. He explains that he stays in the main building – 'the House', he calls it – and that students don't go there. I might occasionally notice visitors arriving from the city. They use the House to discuss business, but they don't interact with the students down below. Finally, he suggests that we begin with an hour's practice tomorrow morning. Then he will give me further points to focus on when I train by myself later in the day. Also, there are chores.

***

James must know that I have had training but he gives no hint, and I do not mention it. It is easy for a practised eye to assess another person's expertise, and – no surprise – I see straight away that James is very good. He is about six feet tall, and at first I thought he was slight. But as soon as he took a deep horse stance, I saw how strong he is. Also, he is in better shape than I am. My horse stance is not bad but I am out of practice, and it is not good enough. Soon my legs are screaming.

***

What is supposed to happen? I tell myself that the fact that there is so little explanation has to be part of the plan. I remember my first, six-week ordeal at the garage. I suppose this is how they do things. Either I stick at it or I don't.

***

Four days. I am exhausted. Two hours' training a day – once with James, once by myself. Actually, it works out to more like three hours. I need to concentrate on the horse stance until I can hold it for half an hour. Otherwise, we focus on the basic strikes, kicks, and general conditioning. I cook my own food. So far, I have painted a wall, dug a trench, hammered nails and carried wood. I feel as if someone has poured sand into my bones, I am so tired. I'll try meditation. But meditation is not sleep, and I need sleep.

***

Sometimes James works with me on the chores, and we talk about Kung-Fu, the students, the old men from China. I assume that he has been asked not to discuss my personal history, and, to be honest, that is fine with me. Already, life here has a rhythm. I don't think about the future. I refuse to think about the past. The only past that interests me now is the Kung-Fu that was asleep in my bones and is being awakened.

***

Several visitors arrived today by car, to stay at the House. This breaks the solitude and – irrationally – I found myself resenting the intrusion. James says that visitors like these are usually higher-ups in the Shaolin Chan Kung-Fu world. They might stay for a day or two, some even as long as a couple of weeks if they are coming to meditate, or to study.

***

James says that the students are due to arrive at the end of the week. Today, there were deliveries of foodstuffs and bedding. There was a lot of unpacking, shelving, and fitting out. James says there will be eight students. Also, a cook and another helper will arrive soon.

***

I tell myself that starting friction is the hardest – getting a wagon to roll takes more effort than keeping it rolling afterwards. Now that my wheels have started to turn, I'll keep them turning.

***

The students came in a rented bus. They are mostly in their early or mid-twenties, full of good spirits. I will share the dorm with them. It is like a barracks, with beds along the walls. I had been sleeping there alone, and was coming to feel that the place was my own preserve. But now there are eight others. I introduce myself as Philippe, from Paris. I tell them that I am not sure why

I was invited, but I look forward to the class. Their backgrounds are varied – accountant, cook, student, postman. Mostly, they have not met one another before, and they accept me as part of the same larger plan as has brought them here as well.

At the first class, we line up and bow to James, and he to us. Almost straight away I see that my training is more advanced than the rest of the group. As I follow the commands I know already by heart and focus on technique, details flood back, more details than James teaches, though I realise he is addressing himself to the students and not to me. We work through the basics – stances, strikes, kicks, blocks. Of course, everyone knows them. There are a few excellent kickers, and the others are very good. We run through fifty each of front, roundhouse, side, reverse roundhouse, and spinning back kicks. James keeps up a good pace, and I'm struggling for air, but so is everyone. The spots where we stand on the polished wooden floor are soon wet. One problem with sweat gathering into a puddle under you is that you can skid. I move a half-step to the side.

Classes are an hour and a half, and there are two classes each day. The main meal is first thing in the morning, and there are light maintenance chores afterwards. Smaller meals are served in the middle of the day and early evening. The morning class begins at 10:30. Then there is the midday meal, and a rest period until 2:30 p.m., when the second class begins. After the second class there is a snack, and more chores. A further meal is served in the early evening about 6:00 p.m. Students then rest, or practise on their own. From 7:30 to 8:30, I practise with James in an annex to the training hall, the usual facility for private lessons. I take a chance, and ask.

"Anything I should aim for? Anything I need to have in mind?"

"You are here for six months," James says, "and we follow the Tao of Kung-Fu." This is a cliché response, and he knows I know it. But we leave it at that. He then calls all the basic techniques we practised earlier in the day, nothing different. This is what I get for asking.

Ten days have passed. We have ground out hundreds, thousands, of repetitions. Today, break-falls and take-downs are a welcome change, bruising rather than exhausting.

During our individual lesson, James introduced sticking-hand techniques, which I had not seen before. The idea is to stand in an offensive position facing a partner. Both of you have the lead hand extended, and the backs of the hands touch lightly. With an easy circular motion using very little force, one partner delivers a knife hand towards the neck of the other, who maintains contact with the advancing hand, following the circular motion so that the advancing hand is deflected and the blow is returned in the opposite direction. The exchange continues in an unbroken circle. Contact is light, and the force constant. Soon the bodies begin to sway back and forth in rhythm with the motion of the hands. Eventually, you begin to feel the gradations of pressure, the precise weight behind the advancing hand as well as the counterweight needed to guide it away and back. You do not so much block as deflect, and everything depends on the right amount of pressure, the right amount of weight, a feel for the direction of the energy. James says we will practise this a lot. He says there are many variations, whether we use one or two hands, change the direction of the movement, or increase its complexity. "This is an introduction to trapping range. But it will also teach you about groundwork," he says. "On the ground, conserving energy is the first rule, and the less force you use the better. Getting the feel of the opponent's energy, being sensitive to small movements and the intent behind them is important in groundwork, and sticking hands teaches you that."

***

One week to go until the end of the session, and then the students will leave. We have covered a lot – stances, strikes, kicks, blocks, the elementary *kuen*, combination techniques, break-falls, takedowns, groundwork, knife-defence. The students were well versed before they came, and the practice was aimed at the refinement of technique. Before and after class, and sometimes during it, James corrects details or makes small alterations to adapt a technique to a student's needs or body-type. It is a strange paradox that the repetition of a uniform practice should gradually produce an individual style, and that this should happen not because a person wants it to – indeed, the reverse. Only if you attend to getting the technique or the *kuen* correct for its own sake, will it, in turn, adapt itself to you. True style is unselfconscious.

Sticking-hand practice continues. After a while, you come to feel almost in a dream, as the soft force of the guiding hands takes over. And yet, not just soft but a softness containing a precisely judged resistance, using the power of a fulcrum capable of shifting a large amount of weight with a correctly applied, small counter-weight.

Today, James adds a further step. We assume facing bow stances and I deliver a thrust punch with my right hand, at fifty per cent of full power. James counters with an outside forearm block. But when he blocks, he keeps contact, and, turning his wrist he sweeps my extended arm down and then round in a circle, flipping it across my body on my left side and spilling me off balance. Everything after the block depended on the sticking hand, and I had not expected that. The combination of a hard block and a soft technique clearly had an effect far more efficient and effective than the sum of its two parts.

***

The students are gone. I have been here six weeks. I have questions, but I recall what I learned about meditation – you can't stop the distractions, but it is best not to dwell on them, and to attend instead to the task in hand. So I leave the questions aside.

The dorm is quiet. I had become used to the camaraderie

and I miss it. But now there is more time to meditate – though James says not longer than half an hour per day. There is time also to walk across the fields and bathe in the cool, moist air of the copses. From the farm, the hills appear close or distant, and they are sometimes invisible, depending on the light, or if there is rain or mist, or how warm the day is. I enjoy the shifts, the feel of impermanence and calmness together.

James will be leaving soon, for a week. He says that visitors will come to the House, but I needn't be concerned. Also, supplies will be delivered, and I should sign for them. He gives me some books, in Chinese and English. "To keep up your Chinese," he says, "and for enjoyment." Among them is a copy of Chuang-Tzu and *The Razor's Edge*, by Somerset Maugham. "Dig deep with the horse stance for half an hour every other day," he tells me. "Remember the sequences of all you have learned. Meditate a little." He speaks directly, cheerfully. I admire him as a teacher, and a practitioner. I wonder what his story is.

***

James leaves, and, as he said, visitors come and go. The deliveries arrive on schedule, and I sign. Two workmen turn up to fix the gutters at the House, and to install new tiles. For the most part, I am left to myself. I read, train, meditate, walk. The month with the students was harder than I thought at the time, and now the body has a chance to recover, to become stronger in the places worn down by the hard work.

***

The new group arrived today, and so we begin again. There are eleven. It is interesting how a collection of people can have a personality – in the same way, I suppose, as cities do. With this group, a boisterous camaraderie developed almost at once – not exactly my style, but I find myself forcing a bit of extra cheerfulness in order to fit in. These students ask a lot of questions, and I tell them what I know. I am visiting for six months, from Paris; I train with the students when they come; I take lessons from the instructor, James. If pressed, I tell them that I don't know anything more. Which is true.

It is good to get back to the class, to be taken up again by the rhythm of the techniques, the metronome of commands, to discover again how, when a skill is repeated often, it comes to be performed in a relaxed manner that, paradoxically, brings an increase in power. This time, I am less tired. Recovery is easier. In the evenings, conversation with the students is mostly about Kung-Fu. I find that I am consulted quite a bit on points of detail.

James and I continue with the sticking-hand exercise. Sometimes we practise with our eyes closed – either both of us or one at a time – so that the movements, the pressure and resistance, are interpreted by touch alone. Also, we intersperse the sticking-hand drills with a new *kuen*, using a staff. James explains that the movements of the staff cover all its main strikes and defences. These are co-ordinated into an almost acrobatic display, combining great intricacy and power. When James performs the *kuen*, the staff seems to take on a life of its own, swooping and scything, thrusting and curving into further arcs and circles until James seems to stand at the centre of a vortex, taken up into the design and intent of the *kuen* itself.

"Usually," James explains, "we teach techniques first, and then the form. But with the staff, we teach the form first. This is because we do not teach actual combat with the staff. We want you to get the feel of it, to have an understanding of what it can do and how it moves, because knowing this makes it easier to defend against it should need arise. The form is also excellent for developing co-ordination, and, as you'll see, it can be tiring to perform the whole thing with speed and power. Your stamina will improve."

As with all the forms, we learn step by step – a small section first, then many repetitions, followed by another section. I had forgotten that in learning a *kuen* the mind becomes tired even though the body is hardly taxed at all. This is why instruction has to proceed piecemeal. If you try to learn too much at once, you become confused and lose everything. James avoids this overload by inserting short sessions with the staff into our sticking-hands practice. Also, he explains that the staff and sticking hands go well together.

"Both depend on the feel of the movements. With the staff, we want you to have knowledge of the movements but we do not focus much on their application; with sticking hands, you can only learn the movements through their application. And so, for now, the feel of the movement is the thing to focus on."

***

One week left. We have been spending a lot of time on groundwork. James is right – because of the sticking-hand exercises, I find it easier to relax on the ground and to assess an opponent's moves by feel, without expending energy. As always, the first lesson, yet again – conserve, defend while relaxing, encourage your opponent to work, stay calm and avoid being caught.

The staff form improves. After a week, I have the sequence memorised. After that, repetition, attention to detail, finding the rhythm.

***

The second group has gone, and, as before, James also leaves. He tells me he is going to visit his family and friends in the city, and there is also Kung-Fu business to attend to. I have plenty to keep me going. Again, I am caretaker and custodian, and the House is far enough back that I ignore it, and embrace the solitude.

***

The next group – already. Time goes, quick as a dream. Nine of them, eager to start. For them, it is new; for me, familiar. Familiar, maybe, but I feel the anticipation.

***

In the lessons with James, I am learning new hand strikes to complement the sticking-hand exercises. These are temple and reverse temple punches, hooking punches, helmet-crushers, butterfly, swinging, and double punches, as well as hidden-arm techniques. They are performed with a twist of circular motion added to the direct line of the strike. The additional degree of complexity makes them versatile and unpredictable.

Also, James introduces the idea that low kicks from a neutral position are often the most practical and effective in crisis situations. Low kicks are basically the same as high kicks, but are kept within a shorter range, closer to the opponent. High kicks take a lot of energy and require considerable athleticism to perform well. By contrast, low kicks are economical, tighter, quicker. James says that the most advanced *kuen* contain low rather than high kicks, because, at the most advanced levels, extravagant movement and athleticism are less significant.

***

There is some sadness always when students leave. James tells me that another group will arrive in four weeks, and, until then, he and I are to work on a new form, a master form, the Dragon form. When the next group arrives, twenty-three weeks will have gone by since I began here, and if I am to stay for six months, I will have only one week left after the new students come. Is the Dragon *kuen* a finale, a seal that James is putting on our time together? The fact that he is not taking his usual break to the city suggests that this might be the case.

***

As usual, James shows me the form to give me a sense of it, and, as usual, seeing it done well is impressive, breathtaking even. I recognise many of the elements, but the variations and adaptations express a distinctive attitude, an entire manner of being in the world, as it were. The central dynamic is fierce and direct, but tempered by a pattern of recoiling movements that never come fully to rest, flowing instead back by way of intricate circular feints that open on new, unexpected, straight lines of force. The Dragon is full of surprises, with fast, low kicks and powerful hand strikes. It is as fluid and continuous as water, and then by turns furious, like fire.

We begin, step by step, first to get the main movements and the broad idea. It is a long form, and it will take time to memorise. When the whole sequence is learned, we will, as usual, attend to the details, to small adjustments that, once integrated, lift the performance to another level.

***

Two sessions now on the Dragon each day. Again, the mind gets tired more quickly than the body, and so, as he did with the staff, James breaks up the form with sessions of sticking hand.

Today, I mentioned that I realise our time is running out, and James answered directly, in his usual manner. But what he said was unexpected.

"Now that you bring it up, yes, it is time to be thinking," he said. "So, I can tell you that on the day after the new students leave you have an invitation to visit the House. I will bring you – unless you prefer to decline."

"Who is at the House?"

"Some of the people who arranged for you to come here.

They would like to know if you had a good experience. But today we still have the Dragon – also part of the experience."

"Of course," I say. But my mind is already elsewhere.

***

As arranged, I go with James to the House. As we get closer, I realise that it is larger than I thought. It has two stories, and an annex at the back. We go in, and James shows me around. As with Sifu's first Hong Kong school, some small rooms have been enlarged by taking out the dividing walls. This, in turn, has required the load-bearing structures to be reinforced by way of a grand interior hardwood arch, beautifully decorated with carved birds and flowers. The result is a large, pleasant, open room at the centre of the building, tastefully supplied, as usual, with traditional Chinese furniture. Rosewood and teak chairs and tables, fine carpets, silk throws and cushions, create a subdued, opulent atmosphere. Behind the central room, to the left of the entrance to the annex, is a washroom. The annex itself contains a kitchen which is connected to a dining room, also at the back on the right-hand side. A further small room that might be a library or a study has a table and four chairs. Finally, there is a practice room on the usual model, sparsely furnished, with a polished wood floor. There are calligraphic wall-hangings, and, on the wall opposite the door is a small raised altar with a statue of the Buddha, an incense holder, a flower vase, a candle, and a small dish. Cushions are stacked in a corner, and I guess that the room doubles as a practice area and a place for meditation. James does not show me the upstairs, but goes to the kitchen to heat water for tea. I watch as he attends to the first steeping, which he drains, then lets the thickening, fragrant pu'erh leaves soak until the deep amber water gradually turns dark.

"Now," he says, "to the small room."

In the library-study, James pours the tea into two cups. We

discuss the several groups of students, and what my experiences were with each class. We talk about the relationships between hard and soft styles, about the Dragon *kuen*, and the transmission of Kung-Fu after the wars in China. Then, by and by, there are sounds on the stairs, and the quiet hubbub of a politely animated discussion, in Chinese. After a few minutes, James says, "Time to go."

All at once, I am nervous. James walks ahead towards three men who are waiting for us in the central room. As we approach, one of them steps forward, extending his hand. He is Caucasian, perhaps fifty years old, of medium height, with powerful, square hands and brown, slightly-greying hair.

"I am Peter. How excellent that you have been training with us. We hope you have enjoyed it." Without waiting for a reply, he gestures to his left.

"This is Wil."

Wil stands up. He is Chinese, older than Peter. His English is accented.

"Pleased to meet you," he says, with a slight bow. Peter then gestures towards the third figure, who is now also slowly standing up. But I do not hear what Peter says. Instead, I find myself all at once breathless, a lump gathering in my throat, all but overcome. It is Sifu. As he approaches, he turns me slightly, unobtrusively away from the others until I compose myself. We shake hands.

"Philippe, we meet again."

"Let us all sit down." Peter's voice and gesture have the tone and manner of a master of ceremonies. We do as he bids, and sit on four antique chairs arranged round a small table. James says he will bring tea, and then leave us. I am so shocked at meeting Sifu that I can barely focus my thoughts.

"Sifu visits us occasionally," Peter says, picking up on my confusion. "You did not know, and so you have had a surprise."

"A shock," I say. "But, Sifu – how is Uncle?"

"All is well with Uncle. He sends regards. I have a letter

for you. Also, one from your father. You have been out of communication. Now you are back. You and I will be able to talk about your father and about your uncle later. We will have time."

Wil extends a plate of small almond cookies, and with them, a question. "Have you enjoyed your stay?" I tell him that I think I have been doing well, that it feels like home, that there has been much hard work and many gratifications, that James is a wonderful teacher, and my practice has improved. As I speak, I know I must sound rehearsed, a sycophant's response. Yet, in fact, everything I say is true.

"All of that is true," I add, unnecessarily. "But, forgive me, I must say also that I haven't understood what exactly is happening. I agreed to come because Uncle made arrangements and I badly wanted to get back to Kung-Fu, to live with the Art again. But I am not sure if there is a plan, or what really is going on."

"That is why we are here," Peter says. "As far as we are concerned, your stay has been a success. Now we want to make you an offer." He nods to Sifu, who continues.

"Philippe. You five in Hong Kong were chosen as a group. The old traditions were dying out in China because of the war and then the revolution. The masters and grand masters fled, and are, to this day, dispersed across the world. Many of the authentic old traditions are now kept alive in the West. By contrast, the Chinese are turning traditional martial arts into a circus act – acrobatics for entertainment. As you know, in Hong Kong, our group – our school – was part of the dispersal, and we needed to build a new generation of master practitioners. The Art needs to be passed on. But the old monastic way of doing this cannot be reinvented in each new country we go to. For monasteries to survive, the people need to believe in the social and spiritual value of the monks. Without alms from the people and support from donors, the monastic institutions will collapse. Shaolin Chan developed within the monasteries, but when the monasteries were destroyed and the monks fled or were killed, the financial basis for teaching the Art was also removed. On the one hand, the Art is not for sale and should not be taught for money. On the other hand, without money, the Art cannot be taught properly. That was our great challenge in Hong Kong, as it is elsewhere, including here in the United States."

Sifu pauses, and then goes on.

"In Hong Kong, we had friends. Your uncle was one of them. So was your father. With the help of our friends, we were able to rebuild the school that had been closed during the war. But we needed to look towards a strong tradition in the future. And so we decided to select five students and to train them for at least six years, to the level of master instructor. These are the students with whom you worked until you left Hong Kong in 1950, and your training was interrupted. For the past six months, you have been learning what you would have learned if the interruption had not occurred. Now you know the Dragon form, which would have completed your programme in Hong Kong, before you would move on to the higher teachings. Not all five of you learned the Dragon form, however – only you. Everything in Kung-Fu is not equally suitable for everybody. Our choice of five students was made so that we would have different kinds of ability, different body-types. We chose a crane, a bear, a tiger, a monkey, and a dragon. Do you remember them?"

I picture my four companions.

"Hooper is the crane," I say. "Mak is the bear; Krullo is the tiger; Nik is the monkey."

"And you are the dragon."

"I was taught the form because it suits my abilities?"

"Yes. We also have a master form for crane, tiger, and monkey. For the bear we have a special version of a Lau Gar form, with leopard elements. Each of you is the custodian of your own master form. When you learn it properly, it will transform your entire practice in its image, and in its spirit. You are just beginning that journey now."

I don't say anything, I have so much crowding in on me. But Peter breaks the silence.

"You have done well, Philippe. As I said, we are here today to make you an offer. As always, you are free to say no. We are practitioners of Buddhism and Taoism, which means, you must test things for yourself, as the Buddha says, and find your own way, as the Taoist sages advise."

Peter then gestures to Wil, who continues.

"Philippe, would you like to stay with us, and proceed further in your practice? If so, you will need to be here for two or perhaps three years. You will live in the House, and teach classes. James will be leaving soon, and he has not hesitated to recommend that you take his place. Your own training will continue. All your needs will be supplied. We will see to it that you have a small stipend so that you can relax or take a short vacation. We know that this is a big commitment, and you must not rush into it. For that reason, we would like you to return to Paris. We have tickets, courtesy of your father. He will meet you there. If you want to take up our offer, send a wire, and return here in six weeks. If we do not hear from you within six weeks, we will assume that your path lies elsewhere, and we hope that you will flourish."

I manage a question. "After the two or three years, what then?"

"There is always more. As the bodhisattva Kwan Yin reminds us, there will always be more until every sentient creature is relieved of suffering. So, yes, there is more. But it is fair to tell you as well that there would be no more formal training with us. You would be the custodian of a great tradition, and you will learn the ancient lineages and be in a position to teach and hand on the Art at the highest level. In itself, the teaching will probably not give you a living, though you and your students will have whatever financial support can be managed by us. The Art will be a way of life, and sometimes in following it you will feel alone. Sometimes, also, you will know you are not alone." Wil finishes and turns to Sifu, who then speaks.

"For you, Philippe, there is also something else to consider. Uncle is favourable to your Kung-Fu endeavours, but he made sure that you have a trade, and area of expertise, and he is holding a place for you in his business. Whether or not you choose to continue your training, that place remains open. All along, he has hoped that your expertise in the world of jade would support your practice and teaching of the Art, and I am sure that his letter will confirm what I say."

As the conversation continued, the different personalities of the three men became clearer. Sifu was quiet, but his words carried most weight. Wil knew about organisational and historical matters. Peter's talents were executive, and he knew many details about the day-to-day business of running the schools in several east-coast cities. We did not talk much further about the offer that had just been made. But the conversation was lively, sprinkled with anecdotes and interesting stories. Before it was over, I knew, without a doubt, that I would come back for the extra years.

After the meeting, I stayed for a few more days. I told James that I was going to Paris but I intended to return, and I hoped our paths would cross again. He said that he counted on that, and I realised, as he spoke, how much I appreciated what he had done for me.

Before I left for Paris, I had one further talk with Sifu. It was the most time I had spent with him, and in his conversation – indeed, in his entire person – he was as quick and elegant as when he had plucked the falling macaroon out of the air those many years ago, without a trace of haste or self-consciousness. His personality seemed now as it was reflected in that gesture – unassuming, swift in going to the point, and so deft that you hardly notice. He explained how the old traditions were being carried on in a new way in the West, where traditional Christian belief was waning as a consequence of the horrors of war and the triumph of secularism. So also, Buddhism and Taoism in China had become so overburdened by ritual, superstition, and sectarian feuds, that those old traditions had become a depleted force, even before the communist persecutions. Ironically, out of their own spiritual exhaustion and cynicism, many Westerners were able to perceive Taoism and Buddhism with fresh eyes and to touch directly on the wellsprings of those great wisdom traditions, free of clutter. Of course, Taoism in the West would not be the same as Taoism in China, but, then, change and adaptation go on continually. When Ta Mo brought his special version of Buddhism to the Shaolin Temple, weren't the traditions there altered, as indeed was Taoism throughout China when it came into contact with Buddhism? The story of change and adaptation never ends, and so, as it happens, at the present time the West turns out to be a receptive environment, offering exceptional opportunities for the survival of the Art. The debasements of the all too widespread marketplace exploitations of Kung-Fu, and the glorification of violence that goes along with the militancy of the market – these things indeed are deplorable. And so we must guard against the corruptions of an overly-commercialised Kung-Fu, and we must, as always, abjure violence. Teaching is now done mostly in small groups, as anonymously as possible because we do not want to be in the limelight. Recruitment is by word of mouth, and personal contact. Vetting is conducted for a long time before a candidate is invited to participate. Then, the invitation is always low-key, and every opportunity is provided for a candidate to withdraw, freely and without obligation. Of course, we still depend on donors, and in Hong Kong, as also in America, we have received substantial help. But, fundamentally, we can succeed only so long as the spirit of Kung-Fu prevails. The spirit, that is, of non-grasping, and with the intent of dampening the three fires against which the Buddha warned. If that spirit fails to hold at the centre, corruption inevitably ensues, and violence comes close on its heels. These days, Sifu said, we also encourage girls to participate as well as boys. This is not quite traditional – though there are exceptions – but the temper of the times is changing. He expected that there would be more girls and women in our schools during his lifetime, and after that, more still.

Finally, Sifu assured me that Uncle's business in Hong Kong had settled down after the post-war difficulties. When he spoke about 'difficulties', Sifu did so with the slightest of pauses and the mildest alteration of inflection. Clearly, he was not going to talk directly about the events that had caused me to leave Hong Kong, but he wanted me to know that he knew about them. He then said that he hoped we might meet again, and that my old friends send greetings, including Kai. I replied that I was delighted to hear that my old friends were doing well, especially Kai. Sifu was reassuring me. I was grateful.

MASTER QUAN

Philippe went to Paris for six weeks, from the end of January to mid-March, 1955. He did not keep a written record of what he did there, but I assume that his father met him, as planned, and perhaps helped him to find accommodation. He probably met old friends, and enjoyed the city. He had a lot to think about, but insofar as his stay in Paris was something of a holiday, it allowed him to take a break from his diary. When he returned to America, however, he began writing again, mainly to keep a record of his training.

As usual, in the following pages I choose a selection of excerpts to clarify the main narrative, which begins in March, 1955, with Philippe teaching the groups of visiting students, as James had done. He now lived in the House, and furthered his training with two instructors: Peter (whom he had met already), and Master Quan. Peter taught Philippe Wing Chun, and Quan, who was very old, taught him Chi Gong and meditation. Quan also provided reading material, as well as lessons in the philosophy and history of Shaolin Chan.

DIARY MARCH, 1955 – SEPTEMBER, 1956

The House is a world apart – a cocoon, in contrast to the bustle of the kitchen and the deliveries and the camaraderie of the dorm when the students are here. Inside, everything is quiet, at repose in the deep glow of the furnishings, the muted light and the faint, pervasive, drifting tinge of sandalwood. As usual, visitors come and go. For some, the House is a retreat, a restorative environment away from the city, and, for perhaps a week or two, they come to relax, meditate, study.

Soon, I start Wing Chun with Peter. He spends part of the week here, and part in the city. He has business to attend to there, but he is also putting together an instructional manual with historical and philosophical information about Shaolin Chan. Here, he will have time to write and to consult with Quan, the old master who is steeped in the lore and history of the Shaolin traditions. Because of his other commitments, Peter cannot devote himself full-time to writing, and so he will come to the House for part of each week, to teach me Wing Chun and also to work on his manual.

Master Quan lives permanently at the House, and he is, as it were, the overseer of everything that goes on at the farm. He must have been here during my earlier stay, but I never saw him. I suppose he is the wise man who leaves no trace. But now he is to give me instruction in Chi Gong and meditation. Peter says that Quan will also help with Wing Chun.

***

In his instructor mode, Peter is more intense and quieter than in the gregarious public role which was to the fore when I first met him. He is slightly shorter than I am, and I notice again the square hands and strong arms. He explains that James has already introduced me to one aspect of Wing Chun by way of the sticking-hand techniques.

"Sticking hand is the central Wing Chun exercise," Peter says. "But before we begin, you might like to know what Wing Chun is." He pauses, and then explains.

"Wing Chun is a Shaolin art invented by a woman, Ng Mui. She named her system after a young female student, Wing Chun or 'Flowering Springtime'. Ng Mui was a nun, we are told, and she worked closely with Shaolin Kung-Fu practitioners to develop her new style to its full potential. There is controversy about the extent to which Wing Chun was modified by Shaolin Kung-Fu, but such matters are undecided, and they should not obscure the truth of the old saying that 'There are no secrets in Wing Chun'. This means, simply, that the central Wing Chun techniques are few, economical, and easy to understand."

Peter goes on to say that there are three basic forms. These are not showy or athletic, and are not difficult to learn. There are also forms for the butterfly swords, pole, and wooden dummy. Although Wing Chun focuses on hand techniques, there are only three main hand positions. There are two main kicks which are kept low, and again, these are direct and simple.

"So, as you can see," says Peter, "there is not much to it."

We both know he doesn't mean what he says. This is his little joke, setting me up for the patient work ahead. He goes on then to explain the centre line. I am familiar with the idea from my earlier training, but in Wing Chun it has special significance. The centre line runs straight down the middle of the vertically-standing body, and in Wing Chun it is imagined as surrounded by a series of gates which allow admission, or access, as it were. The idea is to use these gates to attack an opponent's centre while guarding your own.

"That," says Peter, "is the whole thing in a nutshell. Not flashy; not even pretty. Your Dragon form is a spectacle, a sight to behold. Beside it, Wing Chun is an ugly duckling. No grand moves, but compact, efficient."

Peter explains how Wing Chun practitioners seek to bridge the gap between themselves and their opponents, in order to get within trapping range. That is, they move in, close enough to take away the long-range kicks and punches that strong, athletic opponents favour. At trapping range – which is where you can touch and block an opponent's arms – long-range techniques are shut down, and, consequently, strikes delivered from trapping range are short, taking a direct line to the target through one or more of the gates. It is important to stay relaxed, and to put force into a strike only at the very end, and then to relax again immediately. Accuracy and timing are much more important than power and speed, and the Wing Chun practitioner seeks to strike often, rapidly, and with pinpoint accuracy. When the body does not anticipate a blow and is taken by surprise, and if a series of blows is delivered in quick succession to different targets, the body under attack falls rapidly into confusion or even shock, and is then all the more vulnerable. Ng Mui and Flowering Springtime were women, and it would be especially important for them to shut down the long-range power of stronger and taller men, for instance, and to hit often and cleanly, rather than depend on the impact of a single heavy blow. Also, at trapping range, sight-lines are restricted and the bridging, searching, and blocking hands and arms – the signal techniques of Wing Chun – take up so much attention that an opponent does not see a low kick coming. This is why the Wing Chun kicks are sometimes called 'shadow kicks'. They are elementary side or thrust kicks, delivered low and from close range, and in the 'shadow' of what the hands and arms are doing.

Because of the short range, there are no long arcs or gracefully extended movements, and, consequently, the Wing Chun forms are not especially interesting to watch. Even the basic stance is awkward-looking – though, as with everything else in Wing Chun, it has a practical purpose. Feet are shoulder-width apart, toes turned in, knees bent in a knock-kneed position, slightly flexed so that you can feel yourself just beginning to sit into the stance, the weight on your heels, hips forward, hands chambered. Peter says this is sometimes called the 'goat-grabbing stance', which is, basically, a horse stance modified to look as if you are about to pick up a goat, instead of straddling a horse. "It looks unpromising," he said, "but it is stable and it allows you to shift very rapidly. Like so." From the stance, he pivots to the left, turning his body around his centre line, and shifting only his left foot to realign himself in a position with one foot forward and with clear offensive potential, yet perfectly balanced. "So." He shifts back to the centre. "And." He then pivots right. "Position is of great importance in Wing Chun, but position is hardest of all to learn. Shifting is the key, but getting the feel of where and when to shift is as difficult – perhaps more difficult – than getting the feel of sticking hands."

The Kung-Fu I have so far learned is mostly long range, and I also know about groundwork, which is close range. Wing Chun is situated between these two, and I realise that if I can learn the trapping-range skills, I will be able to move through the three ranges – perhaps with the coiling and recoiling versatility of the dragon.

***

Already after three lessons I see the special genius of this new branch of the Art. As with many things that look simple, I understand again how true simplicity comes only after a great deal of experience. In the Middle Ages, a pope once commissioned a painting and he asked for samples to demonstrate the skill of the bidders. Giotto is said to have drawn a large circle by hand, at a single stroke and with such accuracy that the pope didn't hesitate. Giotto was his man. Simple in itself, a circle like that doesn't come easy.

Peter assumes a stance, one foot forward, hands open in the offensive position, which is to say, his right hand forward, and open, about the level of his chin, and the other hand back, and also open, about the level of his breast bone.

"Now," he says, "this is not our usual way of doing things, but it will be fine. Throw a punch at my head, and use force. You must mean to hit me." He sees that I am hesitating. "Nothing bad will happen, and there will be no need to repeat the exercise. If you hit me, there will be no harm done. You are acting under instruction, and the responsibility is mine. There is no point unless you try to hit me, and unless you hit hard. Now, when you are ready."

He waited. I threw a hard right hook to his head. He didn't move. I was completely certain that the punch would land, but then, it seemed out of nowhere, his right elbow flicked up and the strike glanced to the side, inches from his head. His blocking arm stayed extended, and with a simple turn of the wrist it snapped into a straight punch, stopping an inch from my jaw. The whole thing was like a conjuring trick. The block instantly became the strike, and the short, straight punch (the fist vertical, as always in Wing Chun) had the weight of his body behind it, because he had shifted a half-step forward at the same moment as he drove the strike in. I was taken by surprise, and I felt a sudden rush of admiration for the sheer elegance of this plain and simple-looking art.

"Everything you will learn was there in what just happened," said Peter. "Very close, precisely gauged, minimal blocks that are returned as strikes, the centre line intact throughout, a correctly-timed shift in position maintaining the centre while providing the forward movement of the offence with a clear path to the target. All in an eyeblink. That block, by the way, is a 'wing-hand'. You have not seen it before, but it is a useful tool, as you will discover." I said I was impressed, but also that I wasn't sure how to defend against skills like that. Peter explained that Wing Chun defence is constructed along the same lines as the attack, and that knowledge of one directly affects knowledge of the other. And so, as always, we must begin with the fundamentals.

***

Classes begin at the farm, and I am excited to meet the students and to get going again with the hard work. But none of that is new.

What is new is at the House, where we continue with the Wing Chun basics. The goat-grabbing stance, shifting, blocks, and *chi sau* (the Wing Chun term for sticking hands) are the main agenda. Again, the movements are not difficult, but their application calls for a multitude of small adjustments based on feel, pressure, and balance, so that what seemed initially easy to learn is frustratingly difficult and elusive to practise. Relaxation, the position of the fingers and of the thumbs as well as the wrists and elbows are keys to the magic. When properly applied at close quarters, Wing Chun techniques appear almost casual.

***

With *chi sau*, or sticking hands, we begin by briefly rehearsing what James had taught. Then, we take the stance, face to face, hands and arms raised and pressing against each other in a variety of positions. I need first to judge the weight of Peter's pressing arm, neither yielding too easily nor resisting too strongly. The initial soft resistance needs to firm up as more force comes against it, but when that force is too strong, an opponent's energy can quickly be turned back against him. For example, if the blocking hand suddenly releases and redirects an opponent's energy, the opponent will lurch off balance and lose his centre. It is all a matter of feel, and of sensing the direction in which an attack can be deflected.

We begin slowly, in set positions. When I press against Peter's defending arm, his soft resistance invites me to press harder. As his resistance then stiffens, the weight of the extra pressure is absorbed and diffused through his rooted stance. But if I decide then to push still harder, he might decide to let go of his defence altogether, suddenly, unpredictably, so that my attacking arm is left floundering in the vacant space. The lesson therefore is to block effectively but also to understand how the block might redirect the energy of an attack. Peter says that, eventually, *chi sau* will become a free-form exercise. But not yet.

***

Three weeks gone, and I am to meet Quan in two days. Peter leaves for the city tomorrow, and when he gets back I will be introduced to the first Wing Chun form. While he is away, I am to have my first visit with Master Quan.

***

Quan's room is upstairs. It is cluttered, yet also sufficiently ordered that one feels that he knows where everything is amidst the piles of books, lamps, incense burners, papers, inkwells, wall-hangings, journals, assorted furnishings, Buddha images, potted plants. There is a rolled-up mattress in a corner, and I assume that Quan sleeps on it. There is also a smell of sandalwood incense, though he keeps the window open to allow an eddy of cold air to come through. He is very old, and slight – perhaps 140 pounds – dressed in a traditional Chinese long housecoat. He has thick eyebrows and a contrastingly wispy grey beard and moustache. His eyes are black, arresting, with laugh-lines at the corners. He speaks to me in Chinese. What he has to teach me, he says, is better conveyed in Chinese because the terms of Chinese medicine and Chi Gong do not translate well – if at all – into English.

"But first – *chi sau*. You have been learning *chi sau*, yes? Let us see."

He takes the stance in the middle of the room, and gestures for me to do the same. "Come." I am a little discomposed. I tell him I don't know free-form *chi sau*, but I have been working from some set positions. "Set positions," he repeats it. "Come." He extends his arms, and I locate them with my own. "Go," he says, and I push towards him. His arm is feather light – an immediate contrast to Peter's – but as my attacking hand thrusts forward, the feather-light resistance strengthens, as if I am pushing on a spring or a willow branch that bends easily at first and then stiffens and recoils. I relax as his other hand pushes towards me, and so we switch back and forth, judging the weight, the right point to yield. I push harder, and Quan's small arm for an instant seems to shudder as he resists and turns his hips slightly in order to push up from his trunk. Too late, I realise I have over-committed to counteract his momentary, surprisingly strong push-back, and when he shifts his hips back quickly to the centre and releases the tension on his arm, I lurch forward as his other hand slaps my arm just above the elbow, and with a push he sends me stumbling across the room. He seems hardly to have done anything. To an unskilled onlooker, what happened would appear almost accidental. Again, to me it was magic.

Quan explains that we will practise *chi sau* whenever Peter is away. But, mainly, he will instruct me in Chi Gong and meditation. Basically, Chi Gong is concerned with the circulation of *chi*, or vital energy, throughout the body, with the aim of enhancing health and well-being and increasing longevity. In this respect, Chi Gong is closely linked to traditional Chinese medicine. But it also places a high value on meditation, which can be thought of as the high point of the practice.

"Think of it this way," Quan says. "When you perform a *kuen*, at a certain point your body is present and your mind absent. When you sit still to meditate, your mind is present and your body is absent. That of course is not exactly the case, but it is not entirely wrong. Opposites remain opposites even as they intermingle as well. You have done meditation already, focusing on your solar plexus and bringing the energy down, just below your navel. Now I want you to do the same, but for forty minutes, not twenty. Remember, sleep and distraction are the main hindrances. If you are falling asleep, awaken your attention; if distractions occur, let them slide by, and bring your attention quietly to your breath. Remember to keep your tongue on the roof of your mouth, just behind your teeth. On the outbreath, concentrate on bringing the energy down from your solar plexus to your lower *Tan Tien*, the 'elixir field'. As you know, you have three of these. The first is in the area roughly below your navel. The second is in the middle of your body, roughly at your solar plexus. The third is at the top of your head. These elixir fields are fundamental in Chi Gong meditation. Tell me how things go. We have a long road before us. Sit patiently."

***

Peter teaches me the first Wing Chun form, *Siu Lim Tao* ('way of the little idea'). It is done entirely from the stance position. Again, the main movements are not difficult, but the refinements are exacting – hand and wrist positions, elbows, fingers. At last I am starting to get some feel for *chi sau*, and I see how the movements of the form will be incorporated into free *chi sau* practice.

At first, the forty-minute meditation seemed like an eternity. I am not sure what I am doing, though I assume that there must be a method in Quan's instruction. The outbreath down to the lower *Tan Tien* has gradually produced a feeling of warmth and pressure that sometimes also makes the genitals tingle. I hadn't thought of meditation as stimulating in that way. What do I say to Quan?

***

During the past three days, the warm pressure in the whole area of the lower abdomen has descended further, down into the perineum. It has been gathering there, on the outbreath, just under the tailbone, and I am not sure whether to focus on the breath or the sensation. Today's meeting with Quan is welcome, and I tell him what was happening.

"Now I show you," he says. "Your furnace, in the centre, roughly at your solar plexus, is warming the fluid, the water, in your lower *Tan Tien*. This is the first step. The lower *Tan Tien* is the residence of *jing*, the primordial energy you were given before birth, and which you must nourish with air and food in order to conserve it. *Jing*, which is also called 'original chi', is your sexual energy. The power of sex and the power of violence are closely bound up with one another, and we must learn to refine and transform them both, in order to liberate their spiritual power. To do this, we first use the warm energy of your living body, your *chi*, to nourish *jing*. This is what has been happening in your meditation. The fiery energy of the downward breath from your solar plexus is heating the cool, water-world of *jing*, refining it to *chi* so that it begins to move. For you, now, it has moved down in response to the warming of the lower *Tan Tien*, and it has circled round to the gate at your tailbone. When you meditate, begin as usual, and when the *chi* goes round to the first gate, focus there and breathe into that place. With time, the chi will pass through and begin to ascend along your spine. There is another gate, roughly at the mid-point of your spine, and one also at the base of your skull. Do not try to force the *chi* through these gates with your breath. Let it find its way. Forcing it is not safe or healthy. When the time is right, you will feel it rise, and, by and by, at the final stage, the refined, rising *chi* becomes *shen*, or spirit. For now, focus your attention on breathing into the place where the *chi* resides. Also – and this is important – if your attention should become aware of itself instead of breath and *chi*, and if you find yourself in a state of stillness without object or subject, stay there. It is a precious gift, a gift of the spirit. We call it 'The Sea of Tranquility'. You will not be able to hold on to it – indeed, as soon as you try to hold on to it, you have already lost it. In which case, resume the meditation on your breath and *chi*."

***

The first group of students has gone. The cliché is true: you never learn a thing so well as when you teach it.

***

At the House, Peter asks if I want to go with him to the city for a few days. I was eager at first, but then the idea seemed less appealing, and I have told him that I prefer to stay. I can use the time to practise the Dragon form and some of the techniques that have been on a back burner since the students arrived. I also want to meditate longer. And I want to work more at my Wing Chun.

***

It has taken six weeks, but today I tell Quan that the *chi* is all the way up to the base of my skull. Now, when I start meditating, after a few breaths focusing on the lower *Tan Tien*, I feel the movement, like a shoal of tiny fish flickering along my spine. Now they are pooled, as it were, at the top of it. Quan says to go on as usual, and that one hour is a good period of time to meditate, because at this stage anything less would not bring adequate results. He says that two hours in one sitting would be best, if possible. He also wants me to use the *Siu Lim Tao* form as a pre-meditation exercise. I am to practise the form very slowly, so slowly that it takes between twenty minutes and half an hour to complete. Attention should focus on the movements of the form, until the mind becomes calm and empty.

"Do this," says Quan, "before each session of meditation. It is a bridge between Wing Chun and a Chi Gong exercise I will teach you soon. Start now with what you know – *Siu Lim Tao*."

***

It is two months. Yesterday, on the outbreath into the *chi* gathering at the top of my spine, there came a sweet, warm sensation through my entire skull – a bright, cleansing current, or suffusion. I have no doubt that the final gate is open.

***

Quan explains that path of *chi* up the spine to the top of the head is called the Governor Channel. To complete the circuit, the energy now must go down the front of the body, along the Functional Channel. The tongue on the roof of the mouth is a bridge, and the energy comes down over your head, behind your eyes, through your tongue to your throat, then on down through your middle *Tan Tien* to your lower *Tan Tien*. This movement – first up, then down – is called the Microcosmic Orbit, and once it is open it will stay open and you can circulate the *chi* at will. "Think of the way up as yang, fire," Quan says, "and the way down as yin, water. Now you are to focus on the path downwards, and to do this, it is time to change the order of your breathing. There are different approaches, but ours is as follows. So far, you have used the outbreath to bring the *chi* up the Governor Channel, and that task is complete. From now on, as you begin meditating and breathe out, focus as usual on bringing the energy down from the solar plexus. But when the *chi* makes a turn at your tailbone, breathe in as you bring it up along your spine to the top of your head. As it moves over your head, breathe out and focus on bringing it down to your lower *Tan Tien*. This will remain your method for activating the Microcosmic Orbit – a breath in to raise the yang energy up the spine to the head; a breath out to bring the yin energy down to the lower *Tan Tien*. Remember, do not force anything. Let your attention follow the breath, and breathe naturally. You will find a rhythm – or it will find you. Practise this, and for now, set aside the *Siu Lim Tao*. Next time, I will begin teaching you Bone Marrow Washing. It is the oldest Chi Gong exercise, going back to Ta Mo. Of course, the original form has been lost, but we like to think that our practice is still connected to Ta Mo – in the spirit of Ta Mo, let us say. Today, there are hundreds, thousands of varieties of Chi Gong, and the same is true of martial arts styles. But I will teach you this one sequence, and, as you will see, it will tie in with everything else that you already know."

***

I visit Quan regularly. Peter says that the Bone Marrow Washing sequence is an extension of what I am learning in Wing Chun. This is why Quan had me use *Siu Lim Tao* to prepare for meditation. Bone Marrow Washing is a set of movements, each held for a specific number of breaths. It is like a slow, extended *kuen*, starting at the crown of the head and working down to the soles of the feet. The main idea is to enhance the flow of *chi* throughout the body, and it takes approximately half an hour to complete. I am to perform it each day directly before meditation, and by and by, I am to spend more time in meditation. Meanwhile, I should practise the Microcosmic Orbit until the energy runs freely and the breath is properly adjusted.

***

It is not difficult now to co-ordinate the breath and the flow of *chi* in the Microcosmic Orbit, and, occasionally, I experience still moments when the meditation seems to take care of itself and I am aware neither of breath nor *chi*. There is only pure attention, beyond time and space – the Sea of Tranquillity. When these still moments pass, I return to the Microcosmic Orbit. Quan says that because I am comfortable now with the circuit I should spend only the first ten minutes on this aspect of the practice. For the rest of the time, I should focus on gathering energy in the lower *Tan Tien*. This means concentrating the breath and attention on the lower belly, the great reservoir of refined *chi*, in order to build it up. I should spend perhaps two months doing this. "You will feel the power growing slowly," Quan says. "Be patient. At the end of each session, circulate the *chi* several more times, bringing it down at the end to the lower *Tan Tien*. As always, stay with the still moments when they happen."

And so I move between the students, my Dragon practice, Wing Chun, Chi Gong, and meditation, and I begin to understand within myself and not just as an idea, how the external yang world of hard Kung-Fu and the internal yin world of meditation form a circuit, a complementary opposition of light and dark, force and yielding, fire and water.

***

It has taken several months, but now Quan says it is time to bring the energy stored in the lower *Tan Tien* back up to the head. "Begin the meditation as usual, circulate the *chi* nine times in the Microcosmic Orbit, focus on the lower *Tan Tien* for thirty-six breaths, then bring the energy up along the spine to the upper *Tan Tien*, and for the rest of the meditation keep focusing your breath and attention there. When you are ready to stop, breathe the energy down again to the lower *Tan Tien*, where it is stored. Remember, still periods might occur, and when they do, dwell in them alone."

Philippe's diary entries during the following months are sparse. This is probably because his training had settled into the pattern that became a way of life for him during the rest of his two-and-a-half-year stay at the House. On several occasions, he visited the city for a few days of relaxation, as Peter had suggested, but he does not write about what he did there. He mentions learning the two other main Wing Chun forms – *Chum Kiu* ('seeking the bridge'), and *Biu Tze* ('thrusting fingers'), as well as the butterfly swords, pole, and wooden dummy (*Muk Yan Tong*), but he does not describe any of this in detail. There is, however, one exception to the mainly occasional nature of the diaries during this period; namely, Philippe's account of his progress in meditation. What he was learning from Quan was making a strong impression.

Quan says that the work of meditation boils down to this: use *chi* to nourish *jing*, transform *jing* to refined *chi*; use refined *chi* to build up *shen*. When an experience of stillness occurs, I should understand it as the merging of conscious mind with its source. Such a thing can only be known by experience, and here, Quan points to a brightly coloured tangka on the wall facing his desk, depicting the primordial Buddha, Samantabhadra, with his consort Samantabhadri. The seated Buddha is brilliant blue, and his consort, who sits on his lap, facing him with her legs around his waist, is pure white. They sit together on a lotus, surrounded by brightly coloured flowers. Their sexual union is the first thing I see, but then Quan says, "This is what we are talking about."

I wait for him to go on. "The Buddha is blue because he is infinite. His consort is white because she is pure consciousness, without content. The marriage of pure infinity and pure consciousness that you see here is the condition itself of what we are calling, for want of a better word, the still meditation, the Sea of Tranquillity. In such a state, conscious mind is not obliterated, but also it is not identifiable with the ego. Indeed, it is the condition itself of liberation from the ego, from the turmoil and anguish of the three fires of samsara. All our talk about *chi*, *jing*, *shen*, the Microcosmic Orbit, and so forth, is sometimes called 'internal alchemy'. But it is merely a means to an end, and eventually it is discarded. Think of it as a starting point to enable you to focus – like a branch against which a bird pushes off, in order to take flight. Sensations, such as *chi* moving in your meridians and organs, lights dancing in your head, elation or dryness – these are signs along the way, but they are of passing interest and should not be sought after or held on to. In the last resort, they are of no more significance than the thoughts and images that float into your mind as you focus your attention on your breath. Your whole training teaches you that patient practice brings you in the end to a high level of skill beyond the techniques themselves, and, in the case of meditation, to new kinds of awareness and understanding."

Quan tells me this partly in response to an account I gave him of an experience I had during the previous week, while focusing on the development of *shen* in the upper *Tan Tien*. All at once, I seemed to be out of time and space, and a clear white light flooded my head, breaking then into a constellation of tiny golden lights that swayed and drifted into an infinite distance. I have no idea how long this experience lasted, but the after-effects were a feeling of physical warmth and a sense of serenity. Quan listened, but then assured me that the sensations of light and warmth I had described were glimpses only of the more profound state represented by the union of pure infinity and consciousness-without-content. He explained also that books about 'inner alchemy' typically use colourful terms and metaphors to describe the process that brings us to the mysterious condition of liberation, or union with the Tao. "You will hear of the golden elixir, the pill, or seed of immortality, the spiritual foetus or embryo, the great medicine, and the golden pill. There are hundreds – thousands – of texts dealing with all this, and although a particular selection of alchemical metaphors might be used consistently within an individual text, the same metaphors might be used differently in other texts. But in all the really worthwhile books, the underlying intent remains the same – it is to describe how, through meditation, we can catch a glimpse of original mind. This glimpse then is a seed, or a foetus, which can be nourished so that it grows and becomes stable and even develops a spiritual body that can fly free of the material shell."

Quan went on to explain that the language of inner alchemy comes mostly from Taoism. But in Shaolin Chan, Taoism blends with Buddhism, which puts special emphasis on the fact that inner alchemy is a means and not an end. As the Buddha says, enlightenment is like blowing out a flame. It is the nothingness beyond craving, beyond desire; it is a condition beyond conditions; it is a release into the pure blue and white that are not blue and white except in a manner of speaking. Quan then suggested four texts that provide a sound basic understanding of meditation within our tradition.

First, Ta Mo, as always, has much of value to teach even though his writings exist today only in fragments. At the heart of his thinking is the idea that there is no difference between self and other because all beings are 'identical to the True Nature'. Consequently, 'we clearly know that seeking nothing truly is practice of the path', even though most people are in a 'perpetual state of delusion' because they persistently mistake their own desires and attachments for real seeking. In the Dharma, however, 'there is no self', and so it is best to 'wish for nothing'. Liberation, equanimity of temperament, and freedom from anxiety follow from practising the Dharma, which means being in a state of mind that is also no-mind, and in which we 'solicit nothing' and are 'attached to nothing'.

Quan's second text is the Buddhist *Diamond Sutra*. It also offers a radical critique of the grasping ego, going on even to suggest that, in the end, teaching is itself a futile activity. There is nothing to be taught because there is 'not anyone' who is liberated, and language is merely a means of conveyance, like a raft. As such, language is a mode of mind, but 'modes of mind are not mind', and so, in the spirit of no-teaching, we need to abandon the raft of language altogether. Otherwise, we will remain caught up in delusions, like the vast majority of people.

For Ta Mo and the *Diamond Sutra*, transcendence of the ego and the surrender of its cravings open upon the mystery from which we emerge when we are born, and to which we return when we die – or when we die to ourselves in meditation. Quan said that these texts are the foundation on which the entire practice of Chi Gong and of Kung-Fu stand. He then moved to his third recommendation.

The Jade Emperor's Mind Seal Classic deals with the 'three treasures' of *jing, chi,* and *shen*. These are the means by which we create a spiritual embryo, and everyone is capable of doing this, because 'within each person is a mysterious female'. The embryo is also called a spiritual 'seed', which in turn is a medicine, or 'elixir' which cures us of suffering. 'It is not white and not green', which is to say, it transcends the opposition between the Green Dragon or yang force, and the White Tiger or yin force, and it has the power to open our minds to original mind. When this occurs we are to 'keep to nonbeing yet hold on to being' and here, again, we encounter the idea that there is a state of mind that is also no-mind, a mysterious communion of pure infinity and pure consciousness. Whenever we catch a glimpse of original mind, we are said to 'reverse the light', so that our mind remains aware even as it is taken up into its own primal source.

The fourth book is *The Secret of the Golden Flower*. Quan says I should read it often and think about it carefully because it contains the essence of Taoist alchemy (as in *The Jade Emperor's Mind Seal Classic*) and of Chan Buddhism (as in Ta Mo and the *Diamond Sutra*). Also, it addresses the needs of people living ordinary lives in the world, rather than specialised adepts, whether Taoist sages or Buddhist monks.

The Secret of the Golden Flower uses a mix of Taoist alchemical ideas, such as *jing, chi,* and *shen*, the golden pill, the embryo, the pearl, and the yellow court, among others. Throughout, these terms are a way of engaging us with the governing idea of 'turning the light around', which, as in *The Jade Emperor's Mind Seal Classic*, occurs when consciousness becomes aware of and dwells in its source. At first, this awareness is intermittent, and the initial glimpses are again compared to an 'embryo'. With practice, these glimpses are stabilised, and the alchemical techniques then assist in the embryo's development. But, as before, this inner alchemy is a means to an end, and a discussion of the relationship between conscious spirit and original spirit returns us to the Samantabhadra-Samantabhadri paradox – that is, in becoming aware of its source, consciousness is not obliterated. 'Deliberate meditation is the light of consciousness', but this consciousness 'is neither inside nor outside the self'. Proof comes by experience, and we are to discover these things for ourselves: 'keep it confidential and work it out'. We are assured also that we can do this within the day-to-day world, while pursuing our ordinary occupations. 'So don't stay in your room. Work on the way, whatever you are doing'.

This conversation – or set of conversations – with Quan occurred towards the end of Philippe's training, and is a fitting preface to his rejoining the ordinary world after his three years at the farm. Throughout his stay, he received a small number of letters, intermittently, from his father and uncle. One of these, from Uncle, arrived approximately three weeks before Philippe was due to leave, in mid-September, 1956.

My dear Philippe,

This letter will be delivered to you shortly before your training comes to an end. From the start, your father and I, as well as Sifu, have been interested in your progress and we hope, by and by, to learn more about your own understanding of it. Meanwhile, we congratulate you on your commitment and perseverance. But now that it is time for you to come back into the busy world, we have a suggestion. As always, it is for you to choose what you might prefer to do.
    The business in Hong Kong has gathered momentum steadily since the war, and we are now doing well. Your knowledge of the trade would be, as ever, a valuable asset, and so a place stays open for you here, as promised. The terms will be favourable, and there would be travel, if you

like. As you know, jade is not just a precious stone. It is part of the fabric of China itself, including the Art that you have been learning. For my own part, I did not choose a career in jade only to make money, but also to stay mindful of what jade means, and to convey something of that value as far and wide as possible. With Kung-Fu it is the same. Your knowledge will affect all you do, even though you might never declare yourself to the world as a Kung-Fu practitioner. The good that one does is better done anonymously, and a true bodhisattva is indifferent to rewards or acknowledgements of merit.

So, Philippe, would you consider returning to the old house, and to the business? You are now ready to learn about the lineages from Sifu, and to begin teaching in the Hong Kong school. Let me know what you decide. For now, congratulations, Dragon Master.

Yours affectionately,
Uncle

In the circumstances, it is scarcely surprising that Philippe did indeed choose to return to Hong Kong, where a new phase of our story begins. A diary entry pertaining to his departure from the United States in 1956 is worth citing because it provides helpful information about his state of mind just prior to taking his leave. Although he had learned a great deal from Peter, whom he admired and respected, he had developed a special affection for the old wise man, Quan.

DIARY SEPTEMBER, 1956

I saw Master Quan today, to wrap things up and to thank him. He was the same as ever – quiet, yet radiating an energy at the centre of which he remained always unperturbed. I, on the other hand, was in a turmoil, torn between sadness and gratitude, affection and resignation, confidence and uncertainty about what was to happen next. To my surprise, I found myself saying some of this straight out.

"I am anxious about what happens now, Master Quan. There are things in my past. I have not put them right, and I am worried about what I will find when I leave." Quan took his time.

"To be in the body is to accept misfortune. The sage Lao Tzu tells us that. He also says that destiny does not force the direction of events but merely opens doors that a person can go through. So, choose the door that you believe will enhance your life, and if you seek the way with good intentions, the way is everywhere. Then you can let your anxieties rise and pass by, like distractions in your meditation. Do not deny what they are, but bring yourself back to the task in hand and they will drift away like mist, without taking hold of you. Remember, you have the tools, Dragon Master, to do good in the world, to help to relieve the suffering of others. All your practice, whether it is the horse stance or sticking hands or Chi Gong, is part of the same process, the process of cultivating *chi* to refine *jing* and then to raise refined *jing-chi* to *shen*. The blind energies that lie deep in us and take hold of us through anger and lust then are raised to consciousness, so that we can better understand and transform them. We are not to deny the forces that lie deep in the belly. We work things out consciously in our head, and our head and belly are not divorced from our heart, which is the centre of our emotions, situated between blind passion and pure spirit. Nonetheless, the power in our lower *Tan Tien* is the basic life force, and we must accept and cultivate it. We are complex creatures. We do not find our way without pitfalls and mistakes."

"I know what it is to give in to violence. I regret it. I have kept regretting it."

"Do not regret it any longer. That is futile and self-serving.

You have learned to understand, and you have worked now for years to enable that understanding to develop and to burn new habits into your belly and muscles and bone marrow and brain. One day, you might have to refuse violence again, and even to return violence to its source in order to refuse it. But when the *chi* of righteousness is with you, there will be no blame or guilt if you use your skills. Also, when you have the *chi* of righteousness, an enemy is afraid of you because he knows that you are a dead man already. Dead, because nothing else matters than turning around the light towards the source which is also turning the enemy's hatred, likewise, back to its source. This is the way of Kung-Fu."

I have an urge to tell him about Anya, about that other defeat, that humiliation. But I check myself. This is not the place. And then Quan speaks again, and what he says causes me to wonder about how much he already knows.

"Here, you have learned the ways of the tradition founded by Ta Mo. Like all men, he was not perfect. He was prickly, opinionated, fearless. But he was also patient, persistent, unwavering. In our tradition, we also revere the bodhisattva Kwan Yin, the compassionate one. Her willow branch and healing salve, her gentleness and flexibility are a complement to Ta Mo, and we must learn about her too, the 'mysterious female'. For this, there are other teachings. The way that is wayless is always open to our particular needs and choices, and so choose bravely and compassionately, Dragon Master. Many students will learn from you. Sifu's plan to train five different master instructors is now complete, and whatever you decide, you will bring your knowledge with you. This is as much as we can teach you. Of course, there is more. But as you leave us, do so with confidence."

This was my last conversation with Quan – except for the official farewells to him, Peter, and the others, as we bowed briefly and said goodbye.

JADE DRAGON

Philippe returned to Hong Kong, and began to work for Uncle. He also taught at the Kung-Fu school, which had moved to new premises in a large, pleasant house resembling the one used for the same purpose before the war. There, Philippe's path crossed again with his old companions, Hooper and Krullo. The two others, Mak and Nik, were working and teaching elsewhere, but all five were to stay in touch, and sometimes, over the years, they trained together. All in all, it was a happy time for Philippe. As we have seen, for the most part he resorted to his diary when he was attempting to think through problems or resolve a crisis. But in the three years after his return to Hong Kong, he was content and thriving, and for the most part the diaries contain only brief notes about travel, customers, business and the like. Among other things, they show that he visited New York, Paris, and London, and that he spent an extended period – almost four months – in Paris. It seems that he was working there on behalf of Sifu as well as Uncle. After the war, when Shaolin Chan Kung-Fu was dispersed across the globe, keeping the lines of communication open with a view to maintaining an authentic practice was a continuing concern. To this end, Philippe spent time as an instructor and consultant at the small Paris school, which still exists. When I visited and made enquiries, I discovered that the Dragon Master had achieved almost legendary status as the sifu who had shaped the modern practice and philosophy that the school still follows today. But the diaries do not say anything about Philippe's teaching; indeed, they do not mention the school at all. They contain mostly addresses, dates, and names, and it is impossible to untangle appointments with jade dealers and antiquarians from appointments with people from the world of Kung-Fu. And so I was reconciled to the fact that the notebook Philippe used on his Paris trip would not be much help to me. Nonetheless, to safeguard against missing something, I spent time reading it alongside a city guide, a telephone book, and a map. As it happened, the effort turned out to be not entirely fruitless. For instance, the fact that there are three separate entries for the same street address, and that a spokesman for the current Kung-Fu school confirms that there was once a training hall there, shows that Philippe visited the Paris group at least on those three dates. But we do not learn anything new from this. However, in the case of another set of repeated addresses, I did come upon something that I believe is significant, though I record it here with reservations. Yet, if the clues in the notebook indicate what I think they do, then they help to make sense of a further major event in Philippe's story which occurred after he returned to Hong Kong from Paris in August, 1958.

The point that caught my attention is that, seven times within a period of just over two months, the letters 'PP' appear in the Paris notebook, and beside each is a time, always late in the evening. I did not recognise these letters as indicating a place until I saw that they are probably related to a similar, earlier entry, 'Pl. Pig'. This must be the Place Pigalle, reduced subsequently to 'PP'. Then, in the margin, beside one of the 'PP' entries, is a brief note: 'If you find one you like and can trust, where is the harm?'

As far as I can see, Philippe visited the Place Pigalle, the Paris red light district, probably on these and on who knows how many other occasions. Did Paris remind him of Anya? Perhaps loneliness and anonymity prompted him to seek whatever solace he found at those addresses. Perhaps, even, he had already been pursuing these kinds of interests earlier, in Hong Kong. The relevance of this information is not just incidental; rather, it provides a context for Philippe's confrontation with the unresolved inner conflict that followed upon his disastrous love relationship in Paris in the early 1950s. He had not fully come to terms with what happened there, but in due course he would do so by way of a teaching that is not often talked about and is scarcely known even among advanced Kung-Fu practitioners. The impact that this teaching had on Philippe is indicated by the fact that he did not record it as a series of diary entries. Instead, he dedicated a separate notebook to it, composed after the event itself. As Quan had hinted in his remarks about the 'mysterious female' in their last conversation, Philippe still had things to learn about the craving and dependency that had brought him to grief with Anya, before he went to America. And so, I cite the notebook pretty much as it stands. As usual, I have edited the text to clear up ambiguities, and I have omitted passages that I believe should remain private.

DIARY OCTOBER, 1965

I write this approximately one year after she and I went again on our separate paths. We both know that we will never lose each other because we never possessed each other, or ever tried to do so.

At that time, in 1960, I was not often in Uncle's store because my work was mostly in the warehouse, or at home, where I took care of inventories, catalogues, advertising, or in meeting clients, or travelling. Also, I was almost never in the store by myself. Uncle had two salesmen to take care of walk-in business and otherwise to manage the premises. One of these two had called in sick, and I was there with the other, to help out. He was working in the back office when she walked in. She was perhaps in her mid to late twenties, with long black hair to her waist, mischievous eyes, animated in her movements. She enquired about a small jade dragon in the window. I wasn't familiar with the stock in the store, and I asked her to point it out. I then retrieved it, and set it on the counter.

"Jade dragons." she spoke slowly, as if to herself, as she scrutinised the little figure, "are important."

I said, yes, they were.

"*Jade dragons.*" She emphasised it, now looking at me. "Not just any dragons."

"Do you like him?" I asked, to conceal the fact that I felt there was something I wasn't getting.

"Of course. Apple green, my favourite. These double-hook lines are beautiful. He is probably from Shanghai. Modern. Following the fad for imitating the real thing – Western Zhou is my guess, where they were very fond of dragons. Look. Clever. Those trace patterns underneath are worked up to conceal a flaw. He has a flaw. Haven't we all?" She looked up, teasing and challenging simultaneously. Everything she said was correct. Then she asked the price. She said she would think about it, and with that, she turned, her hair falling like a sheet of black water down to the captivating shape of her hips as she left. *End of that,* I thought, attempting to be smart despite being mainly smug. I knew also that when prospective buyers leave there is a more than fifty per cent chance that they won't return. Besides, I would in all likelihood not be there if she did come back another day.

Some ten days later, however, I was again at the store when she turned up during the lunch break.

"A coincidence," I said. "I don't work here often, and now you have caught me twice. Maybe you have been back some other times too."

"I haven't," she said, lightly, keeping a distance. Her hair was tied behind with a scarlet band, matching her scarlet shoes and a scarlet lipstick that brought her small, heart-shaped face vividly to life, so that I found myself staring, not professionally.

"I have been thinking about my jade dragon. I might even take him."

"In the window, then. I'll bring him."

She looked over the little figure again, carefully, as if having second thoughts. Then she looked up, tossing her hair as if to shake off any doubts she might have had.

"OK. Yes, I'll take him. Wrap him up, please." She opened her handbag, took out her wallet, and counted out the bills. I thanked her, and said I hoped she would be pleased with her purchase.

"I will," she said. "Goodbye. Thank you."

Later in the afternoon, when the second assistant returned from lunch, he saw something I hadn't noticed. At the side of the counter – more clearly visible, mind you, to someone standing in front of the counter than behind it – was a wallet. It was hers, of course, and, presumably, being pleased with her purchase, she had forgotten it. She would come back, surely, and I admit I was gladdened by the thought. But neither could I resist the chance to be chivalrous, and, telling myself it was for a good purpose, I looked inside the wallet. There was a business card with a work number. Her name was Li Chang, and she was employed at a well-known Hong Kong import-export firm. I phoned, and when I was put through to her I explained that she had left her wallet at the store, and that it was safe and she should not worry. She said she had not realised that she had left it behind, and she was shocked to discover that it was indeed missing. Perhaps she could take a taxi and come and get it, if the store stayed open late enough. She really hoped we could work something out.

"I'll tell you what," I said. "Your work address – it's on my way home. I'll bring it to you, say 5:30. Tell me where we can meet."

She named a café – across the street from her office, she said.

She was sorry to be a nuisance, but I had made her feel so much better.

It wasn't even remotely on my way home, of course, but I took a taxi and we met. We also had a chance to talk – I felt that, in the circumstances, she owed me a little time. Straight away I saw again how attractive she was, as I took in the slender golden hands, narrow waist, intelligent, quizzical eyes, the same ironic playfulness as at the store. She said that she worked part-time at the firm, that she specialised in personnel. "The details are boring and anyway they need me only a few days a week. Always on call. It suits me."

I tell her about myself, the jade business, that I travel, and how I have lived in Montreal and Paris as well as Hong Kong. Needless to say, I avoid anything to do with Kung-Fu. Time goes by, and I know I will probably have only this chance. So I ask would she like to have lunch sometime. I add, hastily, that she should think about it and if the answer is yes, she could phone, and if no, then she needn't make contact and if I don't hear, then I'll know that the answer is no. I'm fumbling. I am not good at this.

"It's yes," she said. "Believe it or not, I was thinking I might ask you the same thing. And then you said it. Thursday, maybe. Let's meet here and walk a little to another café. They have better lunches. Not far."

Even now I feel it again, the jolt of excitement. Instantly, everything else went onto a back burner – jade, Kung-Fu, everything of the ordinary day to day. I told myself I should be sensible, but I knew already that there was no chance that I would be sensible enough.

We met twice more. She knew a lot about Chinese history and antiquities, which was not entirely a surprise given what she had been able to tell me about the jade dragon. When I asked how she knew about such things, she said lightly, vaguely, that she took courses. I didn't dwell on this, and instead I asked if perhaps we might meet sometime for dinner and make an evening of it, so that we wouldn't have to rush away. She said that she often worked in the evenings and it might be difficult to find time.

"What kind of work?" I asked; then, "Sorry, I shouldn't be intrusive."

"No need to feel that. I will tell you. In my spare time I am a masseuse. I give massages – to special clients. Mostly in the evenings."

I remembered her 'personnel' job and being on call, but I promptly checked that train of thought.

"How interesting." It sounded lame, even more so when I said it again. "How interesting."

"If you like," she says, "I can show you. You can be a special client – no charge. Reward for the wallet."

I am not sure how to deal with this. I am a naïf, I know. She sees my discomfort and laughs – a clear, bright flash of delight, breaking through my embarrassment.

"Now it's my turn," she says. "If you want to say yes, come to this address at 8:00 p.m. on Wednesday. If you prefer not to come, then I will take it that the answer is no."

She hands me a printed card, with her name and an address. I recognise the street. It is, let us say, in a not quite regular part of the city, Kowloon side.

"I'll look it up," I tell her. "Shouldn't be too difficult."

Then, switching the subject, she asks if it is more difficult to find one's way around Hong Kong or Paris. She had heard that Paris is well laid out – the grand boulevards, and so on – but once you get away from those, it is a tangle, more confusing even than London. Her resolute change of topic tells me that if I want to find out more, I will have to follow up on her invitation, because, clearly, she is not going to discuss the matter now.

"It is always easy to get lost in a city like that," she says. "In Hong Kong too – even more so." She smiles, her eyes glancing, reading me. I am uncomfortable again, but I follow her lead, and to ease things into the new direction, I tell her about some of my favourite places in Paris and London. Soon we are back to the thousand things that make up our usual conversation.

Later, when I looked again at the date and time on Li's card, I realised that I was to be at a business dinner with Uncle that evening, to meet a buyer from Indonesia. I had detailed knowledge of our holdings from the Qing dynasty, in which the buyer was interested, and so I wouldn't be able to visit Li even if I wanted to. I was disappointed, but, I have to admit, I felt some relief at not having to choose. I recalled how in a similar situation once before I followed up on an invitation in a café, with disastrous results. The conversation then was also about Chinese antiquities, and, yes, I got lost all right. Freud says that a neurosis is a behaviour that won't take its place in the past, but goes on repeating itself until it is brought to consciousness and understood. The repressed returns. Li's invitation felt like the return of something all too familiar, and more than a little threatening. She had said that if I didn't turn up, she would know the answer is no. Now Fate had decided.

The lunch with Li had been on Friday, and the appointment on her card was for the following Wednesday. Then, on Monday, Uncle out of the blue announced that the meeting with the Indonesian customer had to be postponed, and would be re-scheduled for the following month. "He is still interested. It will be worth the wait."

Increasingly, I had been doing preparatory work for Uncle, of the kind that he would formerly have done himself. It was good to be relieving him of some of that burden, and to see him more relaxed, more free to enjoy the wonderful environment he had created in the house before the war and then had re-created after it. The house was now once again an enchanted realm, an encyclopaedia of mythology, history, art, at once beautiful and instructional. I was glad to see Uncle enjoying it and being not as driven as he once was, and I did not give the cancellation a second thought. Instead, I focused again, with growing anticipation, on where I would be on Wednesday evening.

In the event, I made sure to allow plenty of time to find my way through the tangle of little streets that I had roughly mapped out in my head in advance, and that I wasn't surprised to find becoming increasingly raucous and gaudy as I got closer to my destination. Although I was uneasy, I have to admit that I felt strangely at home in the midst of that sleazy anonymity, unrecognised among those hordes of hungry ghosts condemned to the flesh and its irrational compulsions. When, at last, I found the massage parlour, it was as lurid and tacky as everything else around it, and I told myself, this can't be true. I toyed with the idea of not venturing further, of not going in. But the thought of Li having something to do with this, of being somewhere there, inside, was too captivating, too strange to resist.

An older woman sat behind a desk in the tiny reception area. There was a cash register, a date book, a vase of artificial flowers, an ashtray, and a telephone. This was the gatekeeper, mamasan, a woman who knew the punters, world-weary, hard as a calloused heel. I said I had an appointment, with Li, at 8:30. She checked the book.

"Down here." She pointed. "Last on the right."

The little room was hot, claustrophobic. In the centre was a massage table, with a pillow, and, behind it, a small sink with soap and towels. There were full-length mirrors on the walls on each side of the bed, and, near the door, a small, wheeled table with a collection of lotions, face towels, a basin, and a large hand towel. There were hooks on the wall beside the door, and below them, a wooden chair. The lighting was a deep, muted yellow, which created a slightly misty, golden effect as it reflected off the violet mat paint of the walls. Everything seemed muffled, heavy with the scent of jasmine.

She came in, confidently – the same demeanour as at the store. "You are here," she said, smiling, amused to be stating the obvious. She hugged me lightly, and kissed me, again lightly, on the cheek. A butterfly embrace, a butterfly kiss. She wore a white, buttoned silk blouse and a long wrap-around black skirt with gold and silver flower designs. Her hair was the same black wave falling straight to her waist, and the same crimson lipstick was a shock, like blood, against the black and white of her hair and blouse.

"Was it difficult to find me?"

"No. Yes. I had to wander around."

"But you didn't get lost?"

"No. Not yet."

She laughs again. I want to ask what she is doing here, what is going on. But she heads me off.

"Relax – questions later. I would like you to see what I do. That's all. I'll need a moment to pick up another bottle for my table – one just for you. While I'm gone, you can hang your clothes on the hooks or put them on the chair. There's a sink, a towel, if you need." She leaves. I want to leave too, and I realise that once the clothes are off I won't be going anywhere. And so I had better go now. But I know that I'm not listening to what I'm telling myself.

When she returns, I am half-sitting, half-leaning against the table. She glances, taking me in. Then, candidly she says, "Better if it all comes off." I had not removed everything, but, apparently, I need to be naked. I do what she asks, turning away from her because of the too obvious embarrassment. "You can be face down on the table," she says. I do as she says, glad to have my face in the pillow.

"Relax, Philippe. Only feel the touch. Think of nothing else, only the touch." She pours the warm oil, and begins. Soon I am oblivious of everything except for the glow of the skin, the warmth of the oil, the hands that know their way exactly. Then, after perhaps twenty minutes – though I am in a daze and have not much sense of time – her head comes close. "Turn over." I do as she says, and as I face her, a soft electric shock goes in a single charge from the entire surface of my skin direct to the core as I see that she is topless. In the golden light, the warmth of the room creates a light glaze of perspiration on her breasts and shoulders.

She is, I almost say it aloud, the most beautiful thing that I have ever seen.

She knows the effect she is having. "Relax. The touch, only." The hands, again, as she soothes, working slowly, gradually down until even the slightest contact at the place where the surge had first rushed at the sight of her, and it is too late. The world melts in the rhythm of the most archaic, the intensest of pleasures. "Ahh!" she says it, almost wondering, and her hands go on soothing the place of the melting wound. "Ahh!"

Slowly, I come back to myself, raising my head to look at her. I see that she has gathered the emission in her hands and is rubbing it on her breasts.

"Not to waste," she says.

"You do that?" I ask it stupidly, and I am not sure what I mean, but then so many things that have passed between us have seemed like riddles.

"All the time," she says. Then she walks to the little sink, turns on the tap, and waits for the hot water. "Time, soon, alas, for us to go." She speaks without looking at me, and when she turns, her voice has a certain impersonality, a new note of self-containedness.

"Come back next week at the same time. I will tell you more then. But during the week we should not be in contact. And if you do decide to come back, no sex in the meanwhile, please, of any kind. Not with yourself, either. And please shave yourself – there. Completely. It will be quite important. Trust me now, if you can. There is much to explain, and we will have time."

She waits as I get dressed and as I gather myself. Then she gives me the same light embrace, butterfly kiss.

"I'll walk you out."

During the week, I could barely think of anything else. I went over the details of all our meetings, every conversation, trying to build the narrative up to what had happened in the little room, to make sense of it. But the more I thought, the more confused and agitated I became. She had invited me to go back to her sleazy den a second time, and said she would explain. I was in two minds about that. I was angry at myself for being on the hook, fascinated, and I was angry at her for putting me there. Also, she had given me instructions, and what right had she to do that? What kind of fool was I even to consider those instructions, let alone to comply? As if to confirm how far gone, in fact, I already was, the urges she had asked me to resist eventually did get the better of me, not because I willed it, but because in a half-conscious dream-state between sleep and waking I imagined her there again hovering over me, and I was jolted awake by the sheer, stunning pleasure of what followed, by its own volition.

As she requested, I didn't contact her, and as Wednesday evening approached, I was agitated, readying myself to go finding my way again through the cramped streets with the smells of food cooking on sidewalk braziers, market fruits and vegetables sweating pungently, unctuous from the heat earlier in the day, and everywhere the clamour, the perpetual din and frantic, strobe-lit frenzy of this part of Kowloon, the most densely populated place on earth, some say. At last I came to the gaudy little emporium, and getting the nod from the keeper of the gate, I made my way to the small, hot room at the back. Soon, she came in. She was dressed the same, and I felt dizzy at the sight of her.

"Here you are," she said. The same little joke. "Well, you know what to do. Make yourself at home. I'll be back."

She left, and I did as she asked. When she returned, the routine was as before, as she poured the oil, and I found myself sinking into the same delicious daze, afloat and adrift on the waves of pure sensation.

"We will go slowly," she said. "You must attend to the sensation, and not to the desire. We are going to learn to contain the desire."

I don't know what she means, but I don't want to break the spell by saying that.

"Concentrate on my hands. Your mind is on the touch. Feel

it for its own sake. Let it be only where you feel it and not where you imagine it is going. Arousal now is the whole body's response, not focused on any one place."

She works rhythmically, steadily, and, as she says, I am present only where the sensation is, where the hands touch, and where the skin glows in response. Then she says to turn over. The sheer anticipation sends the blood running again to the one place, despite her instructions. But this time she has remained dressed.

"Today I am like this," she says, "because we need to learn, slowly."

She stands behind me, working on my shoulders and upper arms. "You might know – or might not – that the pleasure you have in an orgasm is separate from the mechanism that causes your emission. The two responses are controlled by different nerves, different bio-electrical charges. This means that you can learn to have an orgasmic sensation without ejaculating, so that you can have many orgasms without feeling depleted. During the next weeks I will teach you how to do that. It is the first step towards more important things that can also be learned. If you like, we will meet six more times after today. I think you will enjoy it."

I try to sit up in order to talk, but her hands and voice direct me back to where I was.

"There is plenty of time. You have questions. You are not sure what is going on, or if this is a wise course to follow. For myself, I am thankful that our paths have crossed, but of course you must decide on your own account. As always, you are free not to return. If you do choose not to return, I will not trouble you further, and you can forget the whole thing. Otherwise, for now, it is best to ask yourself only if you trust me."

She is in control. In turn, I know that I will come back for the following appointments, and I remember the six-week period when I began Kung-Fu those many years ago. Then, also, I found my way to a back-street location and persisted despite the lack of sufficient explanation. But my mind is racing. This is not the same thing at all, I tell myself, and I make up explanations – conspiracy, karma, coincidence, a greater design. And yet I know, as she says, that I will simply have to decide to trust her, or not.

And so I went back on the following weeks. She said that what she was teaching me she did not teach to everyone. She explained how she would show me first how to block the impulse to ejaculate by relaxing and then clenching inwardly, at the perineum, just before the point of no return. She would use the massage to work up to the touch that had, on the first visit, produced an instant, total reaction. She proceeded patiently, skilfully reaching the tipping point and having me apply the perineal lock and then slowly let it go as the gathering wave subsided, pulsating back into the body. Then again. Finally, the third time I was to let the impulse go, and it did, with an extraordinary force together with an embarrassing volume. She looked on with delight, continuing to soothe, making small sounds of pleasure and approval.

Afterwards, she gave me exercises to perform, so that, gradually, I would acquire control and start also to feel the twinges of an orgasmic response beginning to spark and then radiate, even with no emission. Through practice, the initial twinges would grow in intensity, so that, eventually, the whole body would be in a heightened state for hours, an entire day, even.

As the weeks went by and I became more adept, she began again to work topless. She now took longer, and longer again, before allowing the release, after which she always carefully rubbed the fluid on herself. Then, on the second to last week – week six – we spent the whole time working at the point of no return, so that the orgasmic currents were released in waves until the whole body was charged with a single electric brightness, the radiance of a pure euphoric ecstasy, without any sense of depletion afterwards. As a rough guide, she said, release is advised on a schedule determined by one-fifth of a man's age. So, for instance, at age forty, a man may release once every eight days. It is not good to prevent ejaculation entirely, but it is better still to preserve the *jing* essence.

"You know about *jing*?" I said.

"Of course. It is fundamental. You understand these things. Soon we will have a little more to say about *jing* in relation to what we are doing today."

The next week is the seventh, and we work up slowly by way of the usual intensifying stimulation, easing off, and then intensifying again. By now, I am familiar with the turns and returns of the currents of sensation, of being on the brink and holding until a warm, bright suffusion bathes the whole body as if in some kind of electrically-charged embrace. Without release, I now know, the after-effects resonate for a day and a night, and even longer.

"Let us stay where we are," she says. "Keep the feeling just as it is."

And so we continue, and time itself seems to disappear as I surf a wave of pure sensation, poised on it, feeling its weight, its splendour. But then, after all, by and by I am back to myself in the little room. Before I leave, she says, "Yes, *jing* is fundamental. You know also that in converting *jing* to refined *chi* you bring the golden stream up your spine, and then down, and round again."

"The Microcosmic Orbit."

"Correct. And so I would like you to do one more thing for me during the coming week. Try to bring the sexual energy you feel, try to bring these pulsations at the point of no return up along your spine as you breathe in. If you can, as you breathe out, bring them down again in front. You will need to release the perineal lock at exactly the right moment, but you now have enough control to do this. At first, you might not succeed. It takes a lot of patience, but remember, don't force anything. Especially, don't force your breath."

These of course are the same things as Quan taught me about Chi Gong meditation, but, I tell myself, such ideas run all through Chinese medicine and philosophy, as well as martial arts, and I should not be surprised. But also, she seems to assume that I have already opened the Microcosmic Orbit. Or does she?

On the final week, I arrived as usual, with the usual expectations, though I was also concerned about what was to happen after our final meeting. In the little room, I got ready, and hung my clothes on the hooks. Then Li came in. When I turned to greet her, I saw that she was dressed in her street clothes – a short black skirt, white blouse, jacket, red high heels, her hair tied back. She was carrying a small chair, which she placed opposite the chair already in the room. She handed me one of the large towels, so that I would not feel so naked, and asked me to sit down.

"Emergency," she said. "I must leave. But we have time." She sees that I am disappointed, anxious. "It is all right," she says, "it has been a success." She is using the past tense. Then she talks about what we had practised during the past two months, as if summarising. For once, I am impatient.

"I don't know why any of this is happening, Li, and I would like to know. You said questions were for later, and now it is later."

"You, especially, must be patient, Philippe," she says, not so much to placate me as to suggest that I should get a grip.

"Especially? Aren't all your clients special? You said so yourself."

"Yes, they are special in themselves. But you are special, to me." She looks straight at me, the knowing eyes assessing, reassuring, demanding that I believe her.

"But what now? Do I come back? When can I see you?"

"You have to be patient. Think about what you know. Whatever will happen will happen. Be patient."

She gets up, bends over and kisses me lightly on the cheek. Then, abruptly, astoundingly, she leaves. The cunning minx; by the time I get my clothes on she'll be well gone and I won't be able to follow her. And so I decide not to hurry. I feel foolish enough already, and I can do without the further embarrassment of chasing after her and then not finding her. She had spoken as if there might be a plan, and if our paths are to cross again, I will certainly want a reckoning. But just now, my feelings are all over the place. It is like a drug, this mixture of her beauty, her allure, the thrill of forbidden pleasure, of mystery, of secret knowledge, together with the uncertainty, the mix of hope and apprehension, the strange excitement of it all. I tell myself that at least I have her work telephone number, and tomorrow I will contact her – or turn up there myself, if need be. And so, the following day I phoned. The receptionist explained that Li did only occasional work for the firm and was not there at the moment. Also, sorry, there was no forwarding address or number.

I fretted, anxiously, angrily, through the rest of the day, and, in the evening, however much against my better judgement, I made my way again to the massage parlour. A different receptionist was at the desk, and I asked for an appointment with Li – it didn't have to be today, anytime would do. The woman said she didn't know anyone called Li, and when I asked her to check whatever records she kept, she riffled indifferently through a date book, going through the motions in order to be rid of me with as little fuss as possible. No one called Li was on record; maybe I was thinking of someone else. When I asked where the other receptionist was, the woman shrugged, indicating that she didn't know anything about that either.

I left, feeling that I was in freefall into a familiar turmoil of confusion, grief, panic. The aftermath of Anya was the worst time of my life, and now I was being sucked back into that nightmare of pain and humiliation. But I knew also that, after everything that had occurred since then, I couldn't allow such a thing to happen, and I decided, simply, to deflect the entire cataract of anxieties and questions – the whole outrageous nonsense of it all – by way of a sheer, counter-intuitive resolve to trust what she had said: "Be patient." Li was not Anya, and I couldn't allow the blowback from that other time to take hold of me again just because it had done so once before. That particular neurosis would have to take its place in the past. What I had learned from Quan and from Li was to nourish *shen* by re-channelling the anarchic power of violence in the same manner as its anarchic natural twin, sex. And so I would be patient and I would practise what I had been taught.

The months went by – three, four – and gradually I felt myself on a more even keel, involved again with the Kung-Fu school and with Uncle's work. I travelled on business to London and New York, and on those trips there were Kung-Fu connections as well. Sometimes I realised, almost as a surprise when my advice was sought – at seminars, for example – how extensive my training was, and how I was a sort of ambassador, or emissary, for the Hong Kong lineage. I devoted one or two hours to meditation each day, as Quan had instructed, and I maintained a conversation about meditation with two senior instructors at the Hong Kong school, as well as now and then also with Sifu, though I didn't see him often. My practice of the skills Li had taught fell gradually away. I didn't feel free to discuss them or share them, and my interest faded. Still, I remembered her nostalgically, and I remained fascinated by what had happened, and by what she had taught me. Deep down, I suppose I held on to the idea that something more would come of it, some further episode in a narrative not yet complete. But for now I told myself that the meaning implicit in the events themselves was sufficient, and patience would mean accepting that.

MADAME WU'S SECRETS

Some six months after Li and I parted, Uncle and I were meeting, as we usually did on Monday mornings, to discuss the business on hand for the coming week. As usual, he had a list of priorities and suggestions, and we were to work on setting up a schedule, being precise as always about details, but allowing also for the fact that various appointments and deliveries might be subject to change on short notice. On that particular Monday, among other things, Uncle presented me with a visiting card on which was printed an address in Aberdeen, on Hong Kong side. He said that this was the home of a wealthy woman who collected antiques and had an interest in several of our holdings. Her name was Madame Wu, and would I please visit her on the date and at the time printed on the back of the card. When I asked for some background information about Madame Wu, Uncle explained that his path had crossed with hers many years ago, when she had made a purchase. From time to time, she continued to buy, but she was highly selective. Now she was requesting a consultation about some items in our catalogues, and she wished also to discuss several other, specialised desiderata. Uncle said that I was well suited to address what Madame Wu required, and he was sure that I would find her charming as well as intelligent. He instructed me to answer her questions and provide information, but by no means should I try to make a sale, unless by her request. Her discretion must be matched by our own.

And so, two days later, I made my way to Hong Kong side, to a sedately elegant neo-colonial house behind a high stone wall and fronted by a neatly manicured lawn with carefully tended shrubs and flower beds. A servant admitted me. I was expected, and I was shown to a sitting room, where a small table was set for tea. The room was utterly still, held in the spell of the masterpieces in jade and ivory, porcelain and finely carved elm, teak, and merbau, the densely woven and embroidered floor-to-ceiling curtains and exquisitely finished hand-carved furniture.

Madame Wu came in, almost noiselessly. She was slender, much younger than I had imagined. I see straight away the intelligent gaze already assessing as she approaches. She smiles warmly. Her glossy black hair falls straight to her waist, and she wears a long black skirt and red shoes. She carries a small black handbag, intricately stitched with tiny pearls and sequins.

"Welcome, Philippe. Your uncle speaks highly of you."

"Delighted to meet you, Madame Wu. Have you known Uncle long?"

"Yes. But today he has sent you." She smiles, the deflection neatly effected, and gestures. "Perhaps we should sit down."

There is small talk, as we feel out the rhythms, the potential of the conversation, assessing the contours of each other's language, each other's way of seeing, way of thinking. Then the preliminaries are over. She reaches into the little handbag and takes out a small jade figure. "I would like you to look at this."

I assume it is a test. It is a little dragon, and at first glance I guess that it is modern rather than antique.

"May I?"

I take it from her and move it into the light to get a better view. It is quite nice, well cut, carefully finished. Apple green, even colour, maybe a little pale for my taste. The fretwork is good – better than good – but then on the underside is a small, cleverly worked-over flaw. As I take all this in, I am assessing a price in my head. I don't want to low-ball it, but this is inferior to anything else in the room. I search for a figure, and one comes to me – a figure not far from the amount for which I sold a similar jade dragon to Li, some six months ago. Then it hits me. I am frozen. Stunned. I had sold her this jade dragon, the very one. I pretend to keep examining it, but I am grappling with the turmoil churning inside me. Then I gather myself.

"Where did you get this?" The tone is blunter than I intended, but it suits what I'm feeling, and it carries a note of accusation. "I would like an explanation. Please, Madame Wu, no more games."

"You know this piece?" she asks, waiting, steady.

"I sold it six months ago to a girl called Li. But you know this. Please tell me now, what is going on?" I keep the tone carefully courteous, but steely.

"Yes, you did. But her name is not Li. And yes, I would like to explain to you something of what is going on – what has been going on."

"Madame Wu. Forgive me, but I don't know who you are. And now you tell me I don't know who Li is either – not that I knew a great deal about who she was before. But I do know that this is Uncle's jade, and you are connected to me through Uncle. He must have something to do with this."

"Your uncle has the best eye for jade of anyone I have ever met." As she speaks, she opens into a beautiful, clear smile that is not so much an attempt to ingratiate as it is a reflection of her approval of Uncle. "But you will ask him directly when the time comes. As you say, he has indeed brought us together now, today. Shall we go on?"

She is good at this. Of course we will go on. Taking the initiative, I ask, not without a touch of sarcasm, "Would you like me to tell you what I think of the dragon? At least I know something about that."

"I will guess what you think. It is a sweet little piece. It is well done, but it is modern, not antique as it pretends to be. If you don't mind, I'd like to talk about what it means, not what it is."

"Tell me more, Madame Wu."

"Today, before you leave, I will invite you to come back again, for however long it takes, to listen to my explanations – of the jade dragon, among other things. If you do not come, I will assume that you have decided not to."

"And you will not trouble me further," I say, finishing her sentence.

"Precisely."

She can tell that I am impatient, in no mood for games or manipulations, but she must be picking up also on the fact that I am nervous.

"Well, let us relax," she says, "and so that I can begin to explain, I would like to tell you a little story. I hope you will like to listen to it." Here we go again. Never the straight deal. But all right, then, the story.

"Yes," I say. "Go ahead."

"The story is about an old Buddhist monk and a dancing girl. The monk is called Mu. He spent many years praying to the bodhisattva Kwan Yin, and then, one day, he heard some merchants talking about a beautiful young woman who was attracting large crowds in the city because she dressed up like Kwan Yin and performed a dance. The old monk was angry because he felt that no one should dress up like Kwan Yin – especially not a dancing girl. And so Mu decided to visit the city and to protest against the girl and her dance. It took him two days to walk there, but he quickly found the marketplace where the girl was performing in front of a crowd. When Mu saw her, he became very angry – so angry that he could hardly breathe. He decided to confront the girl when the dance was over, but meanwhile he watched, and the longer he watched, the more he found himself becoming calm, and then a feeling of peace gradually went through him as the rhythm of the dance seemed to move into his body, then through the crowd, the trees, and the sky, until at last a wave of gladness flowed through everything in the universe, radiating from the girl's dance. Mu closed his eyes as the rhythm of the dance carried him into a state of happiness such as he had never experienced. And when he opened his eyes again he did not see the girl but Kwan Yin herself. She was standing on a shining green dragon, and a white light blazed all around her.

Mu was so happy that tears ran down his cheeks and he lost all sense of time. At last, when he came back to himself, it was dark, and he was alone in the square. The stage was empty and the crowd was gone. And so he prepared for the long walk back to his village. But as he was leaving the courtyard, in a passageway under an arch, he heard a faint tinkling, as if tiny bells were ringing, and in front of him stood the dancing girl. 'I know what you saw tonight.' she said, 'but you must tell no one about it, as long as you live.' Then she was gone, and the air was filled with a strange, beautiful perfume. As the girl requested, Mu said nothing to anybody about what had happened. But then, years later, when he was dying, he told the monk who was by his bedside what he had seen when he visited the dancing-girl those many years ago. All at once, the air in the room was filled with the same strange and beautiful perfume, as the old monk passed away peacefully."

She stopped. Then asked:

"Do you think this story is possible?"

"It is not just possible," I said, "it is necessary."

"Ah! Tell me."

I did not consider my answer, which seemed to come of its own accord, as if I had been rehearsing the whole thing already and knew exactly what I wanted to say.

"The old monk was angry because he did not acknowledge his own sexual feelings, so that even the thought of the dancing girl infuriated him to the point that he walked for two days to confront her. It is generally well known that repressed eros finds an outlet in anger and violence. That is an old story. But people can also be unconsciously attracted to the things they repress, and so the old monk was more fascinated by the dancing girl than he knew, especially because she was dressed as Kwan Yin, the sacred bodhisattva to whom he was devoted. The dancing girl seemed blasphemous, a scandal, but she also provided him with the knowledge he needed – if he could accept it – to understand the link between eros and the spirit – *shen*. Without that link, the spirit is arid, empty, a disembodied abstraction, and people who embrace a merely abstract spirituality turn into ghosts, hollow men, witch hunters, inquisitors, haters of love. The old monk was one of them. He was so angry about the girl's dance that he could hardly breathe. In other times and places, gangs of monks like that have stopped the dances and burned the dancers alive. But our monk was alone, and when he allowed himself to watch, he began to discover that the anger he thought was driving him was the reverse side of an erotic attraction that had also drawn him. He needed to acknowledge this attraction in order to discover the real meaning of the bodhisattva Kwan Yin, the bodhisattva of compassion, who, up to now, was just an idea, an abstraction for him. Spirit, *shen*, must be nourished by *jing*, not cut off from it – I know this from Chi Gong. For the old monk, the dancing girl was the gateway to Kwan Yin, just as Kwan Yin is the gateway to the Tao – the great mystery from which we emerge and into which we return. The monk does not possess the girl; he does not possess the bodhisattva. Love is not a possession. It is more accurate to say that the spirit of the girl and the spirit of Kwan Yin possess the old monk. The fragrance – the odour of sanctity it is sometimes called – reaches into the body's deepest, most primitive sense even as, in the story, it is also the vehicle of the most refined spiritual pleasure."

I am trying to impress her. We both know it, but actually, I have surprised myself – even impressed myself, a little.

"How clever of your uncle to send you," she says. Again, she is deft. She approves of what I said but, in order to check my little flash of complacency and conceit, she shifts the praise to Uncle. Yet, she also approves of the fact that Uncle sent me because I have just given her some insight into why he did. Sparring in Kung-Fu is an exercise in getting the ego out of the way, and she is sparring with me now to teach me the same lesson. I see that she is smarter than I am, and I had better take a step back. Certainly, whatever else we are here to discuss, it isn't the jade business. I wait. By and by she begins.

"Thank you for explaining the story. Even better, what you said is exactly what we deal with here, in this house. We teach a closed-door tradition, which is not accessible, or made available, to many. Also, this closed-door teaching is much more about women and for women than men, just as your Kung-Fu world is much more about men and for men. There are women in Kung-Fu, of course, and there will be more. But how many have you taught? Just so, in our tradition there are some men, but not many. Again, there will be more, as times change. Even so, what we teach is not for everyone, women or men. But if you are interested, please come next week, same time, and we will go on. Meanwhile, I must ask that you do not discuss any of this with outsiders. This includes your Kung-Fu colleagues. If some of them are not outsiders, you will discover them. For now, we must leave it at that."

She stands as she speaks the final sentence, to indicate that our meeting is over. And so I prepare to leave. Unexpectedly, she offers her hand in farewell. She is poised, beautiful. I try to guess her age – perhaps mid to late forties. She is slender, like a girl, and with the same fall of shining black hair to her waist as Li. Her black, inquisitive eyes are friendly even as they suggest that she is still enquiring, still taking stock.

"Thank you for coming," she says.

"I am glad to have met you." I mean it.

On the way home, I prepared myself for the reckoning I would have, as soon as possible, with Uncle. He had sent me to Madame Wu, and he knew very well that the meeting was not about business. I realised it was not entirely not about jade, but that was beside the point. And so I went straight to him. "You are back," he said, pre-emptively, with a cheerful eagerness, meant to suggest that he was keen to hear what I would have to report.

"Uncle, what is going on? You didn't send me to Madame Wu on business. With respect – I have to say – I feel tricked."

He is unperturbed. His habitual, fussy agitation continues unabated.

"But that, alas, is in the nature of things," he says vaguely, unhelpfully. "And what could I have told you in advance? What could I say that would prepare you better?"

"She had our jade dragon, from the store."

"My dear boy, the fact that she has a piece of jade that was once for sale in our store is, I assure you, *not* my concern."

In an instant, his tone has shifted. He turns slightly towards me as he speaks, and his words are reproving. I am reminded that, whatever else he is, Uncle is not a pushover. 'Not my concern' doesn't mean that he didn't know what was going on, only that he had slammed shut the door to that line of enquiry. Then, his tone shifts again, as he raises his eyebrows and smiles.

"Isn't she interesting, Madame Wu? I have known her for a very long time indeed, and now you are meeting her yourself. As you see, she has important things to tell you. She has informed you, no doubt, that her teachings are closed door. But they are within our tradition, even if they are not accessible to many of our practitioners. I apologise for my own closed-door manner of introducing you, but it is the best I could do, and I did not entirely mislead you. I know that Madame Wu approves of you, otherwise we would not be having this conversation. If she had decided, after meeting you, that you were unsuitable, she would have talked business. She has indeed had an eye on some acquisitions of ours. You would have told her about them, and she would have followed up. In which case, you might be reporting to me in an entirely different way. When you came in,

I wasn't sure how the conversation would go. I had my hopes. I was quietly confident."

So, Uncle and Madame Wu were in cahoots, and when Uncle says he has known her for 'a very long time indeed', do I hear a hint that he, perhaps, also might be acquainted with her teachings? I realise that he will not tell me if I ask, which, in any case, I don't feel inclined to do. I would much rather talk about Li, but if I start down that path and get things wrong, I will end up being mightily embarrassed. The neatness by which I am hemmed in is suddenly as clear as an unexpected checkmate. "I am confused," is the best I can manage.

"But you must feel pleased and delighted," Uncle says, "because being un-confused would be so easy. You are free to let all this go; to let things return to normal. You have a busy and interesting life which will continue if you don't accept Madame Wu's invitation. I won't send you there again on business, for instance, and here we would go on as usual. You know how this goes."

"I know how it goes," I say. "And we both know I will go back."

"I doubt if you'll regret it. I know you will not. Of course, as Madame Wu has told you, it is not proper to discuss what you will learn. Only when you have become truly an insider, will you discover other insiders."

And so, I kept my next appointment with Madame Wu, and what she taught me in the coming months utterly changed my world.

"I am a White Tigress," Madame Wu says. "The young woman you knew as Li is my student. In due course, she also will become a White Tigress. During our last meeting, we already touched on the fundamentals of what White Tigresses do. Put simply, we practise and transmit teachings about the main themes you and I discussed in the story of the monk and Kwan Yin – that is, the transformation of *jing* to *shen*, of eros to spiritual enlightenment, liberation, and immortality. The key point, as you correctly said, is that we should not deny or repress eros, but transform it, consciously. In your Kung-Fu training, you have learned the same thing about transforming the urge to violence, not by repressing it, but by making it conscious through a long process of disciplined training. This also is the transformation of *jing* to *shen* that is basic, again, to your Chi Gong meditation.

Sex, of course, is necessary for the survival of the species. But think of it, the more prolific nature is in reproduction, the less personal is the relationship between the mating pairs. Frogs, snakes, turtles lay large numbers of eggs that they never see hatch. They never know their offspring. They mate only in order to reproduce. But as the path of evolution proceeds towards the warm-blooded creatures and the creatures endowed with more capacious intelligence, two things happen. First, the number of offspring decreases; second, mating becomes more personal, and the pair more bonded. This is not uniform, of course, but birds lay fewer eggs than frogs, and they bond more closely. Chimpanzees are less prolific than fish, and their emotional relationships are closer. You might argue that bonding, whether with another individual or within the group, is an evolutionary mechanism for coping with the task of raising more complex offspring. This is true, as we see most clearly in human beings. Our most important evolutionary advantage – the brain that gives us language – is so central that we are physically helpless, utterly dependent when we are born, because the pre-formation of the brain is of such overwhelming significance for us. And so, the fact that humans bond closely is explainable on the grounds that the mechanisms of evolution cause us to do so. But then there is the interesting further fact that human beings are capable of a very special kind of attachment that is not dependent at all on reproduction. Many of the world's great love stories are about a relationship so strong that not even death can deter it, and in which reproductive sex plays no part at all. The ancient Chinese tale of the 'butterfly lovers', Liang Shanbo and Zhu Yintai, is an example, and you are familiar with Romeo and Juliet, or Tristan and Isolde."

I am not sure if this is a statement or a question, but I reply anyway, quietly, almost as if recollecting.

"And so, love kills everything."

"Ah! What you say, Philippe, is almost what I would say too. But not quite. The love with which I am concerned says 'Yes', indeed even to the point of death. Or else it is not real. However, this love comes through the eyes, *shen*. True, it is driven by eros, but the generative impulse of the *jing* energy is liberated by the refinement of *jing* to *shen*. As you and I know, this process needs to be consciously developed, and the problem with those young lovers in the stories is that they could not be sufficiently independent of one another, or realise that the bliss they seek, the elixir of immortality, has to be discovered by each of them individually, because for each the way is different. It is not enough for them just to mirror each other. They need instead to reach over, across from their own individual separateness, and in so doing to surrender self-interest in order to raise the other up. A White Tigress knows this. Sex, and sexual love – in exactly the same way as a Kung-Fu form or opening the Microcosmic Orbit – is a vehicle, a raft to bring us to the other shore. If we cling to Kung-Fu as a set of fighting tricks, or to Chi Gong as a means of attaining special powers, we miss the point and are left with a debased and dangerous parody of the real thing we seek. So also we should not cling to sexual love because we will only suffer more if we do. Sadly, in the world as we know it, sex is mostly a primitive business, driven by unconscious evolutionary imperatives. Some of it is brutal, most of it is tangled with possessiveness, jealousy, the desire to consume the supposedly beloved. The world will never have peace until these things are understood, and there might be many ways to enable this to happen. You and I have our own paths, and although we cannot change the world, we might relieve suffering a little here and there – a *soupçon*, let us say."

Her perfect pronunciation of the word caught my ear – *'soupçon'*. I repeated it aloud, as a sort of shorthand question, and she replied in French, effortlessly explaining that she had been educated at the Sorbonne, and, as a girl, in London. She went on then, in English, to say that the future of the Art, of the Taoist –Buddhist traditions themselves, would depend on a convergence of Eastern and Western interests, not only because of what was happening in China, but also because East and West need each other in this venture – in the interests, that is, of preserving an ancient wisdom while also revitalizing it. What she is telling me now, she hopes, is itself an example of the possibilities of such a convergence. She herself is Hong Kong Chinese, but, as I now know, she was educated in Europe. We have that in common, she says.

Then she returns to where we were – to the *soupçon* of relief in a world beset with violence and sexual predation. "In the classic by Zhang Sanfeng, *Gathering the True Root Power*," she explains, "the quest for enlightenment is interpreted in the context of what is described as 'flowers and combat', which means the inter-involvement, the entanglement of sex and violence, love and aggression, that is part of what we are. Zhang Sanfeng teaches us to unravel this tangled skein, and, in the process, to acquire the means of restoring and replenishing that he compares to a golden flower and a golden elixir." Madame Wu goes on to say that *The Secret of the Golden Flower* also explains how we are to refine these energies, so that the medicine will develop – the elixir, the spiritual foetus that symbolises the transfigured impulse to procreate materially. Of course, I am already familiar with *The Secret of the Golden Flower*, but now I discover that it deals with the refinement of sex that complements the refinement of violence. White Tigresses are especially interested in this challenge, this refinement, but they must work discreetly, because of the widespread prejudices of our sexually repressed but addicted world. By and large, the major religions repress sex in the interests of what they take to be spiritual development, and this is sometimes the case even with Buddhism. Taoism provides a counterweight, and Taoism alone offers a set of teachings that allow us to bring sexuality to consciousness. "All of us have wounds," Madame Wu says, "things that make us angry and fill us with yearning and desire. But anger and eros – violence and sex – have to be dealt with together. You, Philippe, have dealt with one of these, but not the other. And so we are here, behind closed doors in the lair of a White Tigress. I hope that you are still interested."

She knows that I am interested, and she knows quite a lot about me besides – from Uncle, no doubt. Also, she is formidable, and I realise that if I go further into her world, I will have to put myself entirely into her hands.

"I am interested," I tell her. "I am in your hands."

She goes on: "The Yellow Emperor, legendary founder of Chinese civilisation, was instructed by the Western Royal Mother, who offers the Peach of Immortality as a gift to her chosen favourites. The peach is also the elixir – the essence of *jing*, refined to *chi*, and transformed to *shen*. It also produces the seed or drop of Yang Shen, the pure spirit that begets the immortal embryo or foetus. As usual, we are talking here in a symbolic language, a poetry that we must read accordingly. And so, the elixir is also the nectar or healing potion poured out by the bodhisattva Kwan Yin from the vase she carries. These female figures are embodiments of the Mysterious Female herself, the primal mother. Lao Tzu says that he is 'different' from other men because the primal mother nourishes him, and he then asks, 'Can you play the role of woman?'. And so we White Tigresses are not the only purveyors of the knowledge of the 'difference' Lao Tzu mentions, but we work within our own special tradition. Perhaps you know that in instructing the Yellow Emperor, the Western Royal Mother had three helpers – Mysterious Girl, Plain Girl, and Multihued Girl – who taught the Yellow Emperor the arts of sexual alchemy or transformation. *The Plain Girl Classic* records their instructions, and we White Tigresses live still in the tradition of the Plain Girl's teachings, which have been preserved and developed over the centuries. Mostly, we work alone. After our training under the instruction of another White Tigress – which is as lengthy as your Kung-Fu training – we go our own way and do not often meet another of our kind. But we find our own young women to train, in order to preserve the tradition. Beyond that, nobody knows who we are, except by invitation. As with you, for instance."

She pauses. I tell her that I am grateful for the privilege, but also that I am not sure how I could fit into a White Tigress world.

"Then let us go a step further," she says.

"Please do, Madame Wu."

"You will remember in *The Jade Emperor's Mind Seal Classic*, the elixir is called 'Green Dragon and White Tiger'. The green dragon here is male or yang, and the white tiger is female or yin. To make the contrast clearer – and because there is a certain wordplay involved – we call ourselves White Tigresses. The main point is that the elixir contains both male and female energies, and we White Tigresses cannot properly develop our alchemy without the replenishment of male yang energy. And so, when you were with Li, after building up your semen, she rubbed the emission on herself, either on her face or on her breasts. She did this because, just as the internal alchemy of Chi Gong helps to rejuvenate and promote health, so do these White Tigress practices. You might be interested to know that Li is not as young as she looks. She is older than you – not much, but slightly. I am twenty-five years older than you, and I expect that you would not guess. No matter. Looking young is a side benefit, and is less important than the ways in which a White Tigress uses her male apprentices – or 'client-apprentices', let us say – to further her development.

As you are now aware, these men don't really understand what they have got themselves into, and a beginning Tigress, such as Li – or a fully-fledged one, such as myself – will meet many of them, but never for an extended period. Ah, I see that you recognise this, and perhaps it alarms you a little. Shall I go on? Very well. Now, of course, you are beyond the level of those men because already you know a great deal more than any of them ever would. Consequently, we have invited you here so that, if you wish, you can prepare for the next stage. In that case, you will learn certain techniques, and you will work with a student tigress, Mei Lin, to practise them. In such a transaction, we regard men and women as completely equal, and the relationship is entirely free of jealousy or possessiveness. This is how it should be in the world at large, of course, but the world at large has a long way to go before our teachings are well enough understood, rather than vilified as they are now, so that we are forced to teach behind closed doors. But I will need to know if you wish to proceed. You are familiar with the routine: if you decide against, then you simply do not come for our next appointment. That is all the explanation I need or want. But if you choose to go further, from this point on we expect your commitment."

Apparently, I had been Li's 'client-apprentice' without knowing it, and I wasn't entirely comfortable in finding that out. Furthermore, I didn't like the idea of perhaps being manipulated in similar ways by the next fledgling tigress who might also be furthering her studies at my expense. I thought it best to say this, and I did. Madame Wu listened attentively, and said she agreed. She apologised for causing me discomfort. Still, she wanted to point out that she needed to be scrupulously careful about whom she would invite into a situation such as our present one. She asked me to imagine how easily things could go wrong, and how badly. She had a point.

"In my meetings with Li, you were vetting me without my knowing it," I said.

"I'm afraid so. But I promise you, should you agree to meet Mei Ling, both of you will have a full explanation of everything that will happen. No more secrets."

When I arrived for our next appointment, the front door was

opened, not by the familiar servant – but by the girl I had known as Li. It was a shock, of course, and for a moment I was breathless, as a flood of emotion rushed wildly, ungoverned, unbidden. And yet, strangely, I was not surprised. It made too much sense that it should be her, as lovely as ever, her face flushed with anticipation.

"Mei Lin," I said, "formerly known as Li." She smiled and looked down, abashed, perhaps, but not discomposed.

"Dear Philippe. It is so lovely – so important – to see you. I wanted to bring you in, myself."

We went into the sitting room. Madame Wu was waiting, with tea prepared. The mood was pleasant, festive even. Both women had a similar, slightly teasing playfulness, and I felt clumsy by comparison. But we talked gladly, discussing the events that had brought us here, various aspects of the Art, language, education, Hong Kong, Europe, and the mysteries of jade. Then, by and by, Madame Wu turned the conversation to our main concern. She suggested that Mei Lin and I should take time to discuss with one another what we were about to undertake. A basic requirement was that we have genuine feelings for each other. Madame Wu said that Mei Lin had selected me a long time ago and would not have left her wallet at the store if she had not been interested in meeting me again. Nor would she have shown me the techniques of retention and circulation of the Microcosmic Orbit unless she felt that I, in turn, was attracted to her and could be trusted. Also, the fact that I came back to the massage parlour after our eight sessions, and had tried to contact Mei Lin at work, showed that I was not indifferent. I had no idea how Madame Wu knew this, but I didn't interrupt. Finally, she said, Mei Lin had returned the little jade dragon as a token – a cryptic invitation, perhaps. And what did I feel, after all this?

I replied easily, unguardedly, saying that I had no doubt whatsoever about my feelings for Mei Lin. I had been sufficiently tested to be certain, but I realised also that love is not possessive, and is without conditions. Nonetheless, I would appreciate knowing how it is that Mei Lin arrived at the shop in the first place, to purchase the jade dragon.

"Uncle," I ventured, "is in on this."

Madame Wu's answer was partly evasive, though no doubt also true.

"The networks are broader than your uncle," she said, "and information comes, over time, from more than one source."

Madame Wu then quietly excused herself, explaining that Mei Lin and I should go on talking together with a view to taking things to the next stage. There would be no rush. We could meet as often as we wished before deciding.

As it happened, Mei Lin and I took up pretty much straight away where we left off those six or so months ago. I felt the old warmth and power of attraction return, as exhilarating and moving as ever, fuelled now by an extra intensity because the feelings were so unguardedly mutual. We talked for a long time that afternoon about our hopes and vulnerabilities, and about the Art that we had experienced together but from such different directions. There was no hesitation about going on, and we agreed, simply, to let Madame Wu know that we were ready.

As it turned out, I was better prepared for Madame Wu's teachings than I realised. The techniques of retention and of transforming *jing* to *shen* by way of the Microcosmic Orbit were basic to the first two stages that Madame Wu set out for us. As lovers, Mei Lin and I should work together with the Microcosmic Orbit, and learn to synchronise our breathing. This would require practice, but, beyond all else, we should remain sensitive to one another. The purpose of the exercise is that the male, yang energy replenishes itself with the female, yin energy, and the female yin replenishes itself with the male yang. For this to happen, the man must be still and prevent release. The woman must be active, and can be orgasmic as often as she wishes. Of course, the man is not denied release entirely, but he must ration himself and the woman can sometimes relax from her active role.

I do not record the details of our practice. Suffice it to say that the results were extraordinary, beyond expectation, utterly transformative. It was like stepping out of some desolate, smoke-filled waste – the smouldering, war-torn, ruinous world of samsara – into a Pure Land of clarity, beauty, fragrance, and delight. The significance of sex then is so transfigured that there is no question of returning to the madness of what passes for sexual gratification in a world that passes for normal but which has merely become habituated to its own grotesque abnormalities.

The first stage of Madame Wu's training lasted two months, moving on then to stage two, which is more subtle, more intricate. The techniques must be learned as carefully and patiently as the Kung-Fu forms, so that, through practice, they become fully embodied. I was to learn again the importance of not dwelling on externals for their own sake, but rather as a means of turning the light around so that the vehicle, the raft that has brought us to bliss and illumination, is no longer necessary. *The Jade Emperor's Mind Seal Classic* indeed says that 'The Elixir is called Green Dragon and White Tiger', but it also says, 'The Elixir is within yourself, / It is not white and not green'.

Our practice requires Mei Lin and me to stay together for between two and five years. After that, we would be free to stay longer, or even to marry and to have a regular life together. As I write this, more than two years have passed, and so we will see. But of one thing I am certain. Mei Lin is the most beautiful woman I shall ever know, and there is no one I could love more. This is so not just because of the intensities, joys, and discoveries we have experienced together, but because knowing her has been so profoundly, so cleanly healing that such a thing can never happen again, because there will never be the need. For the most part, we live separately, with regular meetings and enough outside engagements and activities to add variety. Sometimes, by her invitation, I stay for a night in her apartment in Madame Wu's house. We hardly see Madame Wu these days, though sometimes the three of us meet and talk and have tea. I have introduced Mei Lin to Uncle, who seems entirely comfortable with what has been going on. I conclude that this is so because he has not questioned me at all, and he accepts my absences. I did, however, on one occasion try to clear the air.

"You know about Madame Wu's teachings, and about what is going on at her house?"

"Yes," he said. "I hope you will do exactly as she advises. Madame Wu is a very remarkable woman."

He had said that last sentence before, and now he spoke it with a deliberately gauged inflection that I felt I was meant to notice. What exactly did Uncle know about being a jade dragon? And what was so remarkable, for him, about Madame Wu that he kept repeating the point? He raised his eyebrows, a gesture opposite to winking but with a trace of a wink nonetheless. Or so I thought.

The White Tigress notebook ends here. I have been unable to discover what happened at the conclusion of the agreement between Philippe and Mei Lin. I met him for the first time many years afterwards, and I am virtually certain that he was unmarried. Occasionally, I did see him in the presence of a woman, but I am not sure if it was the same woman each time. My dealings with him were for the sole purpose of learning and practising Kung-Fu, and I knew nothing about his personal life. I have learned more about him from his diaries, and from the enquiries I have made since his death, than I knew at any time before.

And so the story of the Kung-Fu diaries is almost finished. There are further assorted papers, but they are of incidental interest, comprising notes about meetings with his father – to whom, it seems, he became closer as the years went by – and about trade deals, books, appointments. But there is nothing that adds substantively to what he wanted me to convey – namely, a story that would not be just his story, but a story of broad human interest about Shaolin Chan Kung-Fu. Perhaps he was selective about what he put into the box in the first place, and perhaps there are other notebooks, documents, papers. I have no way to know. Still, from outside the box I can now add a few details of my own to bring to an end a story that, as with all stories, is never complete.

Philippe continued to work and to travel in the service of his uncle's business, and also to teach at Sifu's school, as the Dragon Master. Because he travelled, he was able to consult and teach seminars in the cities to which he was also connected by business: London, Paris, New York, Seattle, among others. In one of these seminars, in London, my path first crossed with his, and, as it happened, shortly afterwards I got myself posted to Hong Kong for two years, as a journalist. My training continued there, and was the basis of what was to become a growing friendship between Philippe and myself as the years passed.

In 1970, when he was age fifty, his father died, and a few years after, in 1973, Uncle also died. Philippe inherited the jade business, and he hired managers to oversee it, so that he could devote more time to the Art. As far as I can tell, the new arrangements worked well, not least because Philippe knew all sides of the business and was a vigilant overseer. I have been unable to find out much about what happened to Sifu. The custodians of the tradition in Hong Kong value anonymity, and they were politely reluctant to give me much information. But there are indications that Sifu returned to China, and was becoming 'an immortal', as one of my interviewees put it. In Taoism, 'immortal' can mean, simply, a very old man, but the word carries other implications as well. It can mean a person who has developed *shen* to an exceptionally high degree and whose spirit can leave the body at will, to fly among the stars. Although I could not discover where exactly in China Sifu had gone, I thought of him, as I still do, as a Taoist sage dwelling among the high mountain mists, living on dew and air and flying free in the perfect glory of his liberated spirit, at one with the Tao.

Philippe died in Hong Kong in 2001 at age eight-one, after a short illness. His diaries had been stored in the school in Hong Kong, before he brought them to England on that final trip, when he left them with me. The people at the Hong Kong school were aware of his wishes to have me write this book, which I would like now to conclude with his words, rather than my own. The following account was written on some loose sheets inserted under the back cover of the White Tigress notebook. They are undated. My guess is that they were written after Philippe had undergone his training as a jade dragon, because they make most sense in that context.

DIARY UNDATED

I am to catch a plane tomorrow, from London to Hong Kong. I have two hours to put in before the final meeting with my contact here. It has been a long day. A glass of English beer will go down well, and so I make my way to a pleasant-looking pub I noticed earlier on Vauxhall Road, near Victoria Station where I am to meet my contact.

In the late afternoon, the pub is almost empty. Two middle-aged Pakistani men are watching cricket on TV. The set is fixed high on the far wall, opposite the door. To the right, behind a pillar, another customer is partly visible. I sit near the door, behind the two men, with the bar on my right. I take the beer, and look at the cricket. Mainly, I am enjoying the animated reactions of the two other watchers, and I don't notice the woman come in. She sits at the bar, her legs turned to the left, so that she is also facing inward, away from the door. She ponders her glass. I guess she is thirty-something.

Then the two men arrive. They order drinks but the barman

refuses to serve them. There has been previous trouble, I assume, and now he won't serve them and they are angry. They are in their twenties, roughly dressed, aggressive. One is about six feet, the other a little shorter, and now they are shouting abuse at the barman. The tall one says something to the woman, who is close to him, on his left. She doesn't respond, and he leans over and whispers something, bending closer to her, so that she recoils – "Get away from me." But he doesn't. He leans further in, menacing, and now he is saying vile things to her, so that she slowly crumples under the weight of the vile words. She cannot look at him, only try to shut out what she can't stop hearing. Satisfied for the moment, he turns back to the barman, loudmouthed, threatening.

I have drunk the beer, and I should go. And so I stand, slowly. But instead of turning towards the door I find myself stepping around the table towards the bar. I stand to the left of the woman, not close, and not looking at her. I don't look at him either, the vilifying one, but he is in my peripheral vision. Instead, I look across the bar, unfocused. He takes me in, deliberating, then shouts, "You. Tough guy!" I turn, taking note of his centre line. He steps towards me. I step back, my hands raised in a conciliatory gesture which is also a fence – a perimeter beyond which he can't come without initiating an attack. I am at ease. I have been here ten thousand times, and nothing concerns me except the moment. "Tough guy!" He barks it again and takes another step, raising his fists but not closing with me, not attacking. I step back again, re-affirming the fence – another conciliatory gesture.

"Don't." I say it calmly, no threat, looking straight at him, into him, slightly shifting my stance towards the standard Wing Chun offensive position, though he would not know this.

He pauses, and I watch him deciding. He considers for perhaps three seconds, then wheels and shouts to his friend who is still hurling abuse at the barman. "Hoi! Out of here! Sods!" He strides to the door, waving his arms, and his companion follows, walking backwards, still mouthing threats. They leave.

"I am sorry you were upset," I say to the woman. She is still hurt but now she is also defiant.

"I'm OK. Thanks. Can I buy you a drink, maybe?" She gestures to the barstool beside her.

"Thank you, I must be going. Perhaps next time." She nods, OK.

I return sometimes in my mind to that scene, attempting to understand why it stays with me. Now I am even writing about it, and I can only say that I do so to remind myself that no outside observer would know or guess how much work, how much dedication, how much knowledge, over how many years, went into having nothing happen in those few moments. Again, I begin to understand what Quan once said. The wounds of love and war are healed together or not at all.

AFTERWORD

I was born in London, England, in 1946, the first of the baby-boom years. I was a beneficiary of the 1947 Education Act and I received a good grammar school education, before reading French and English at a red-brick university. My father was attached to the Foreign Office during the war, and my mother, who was a few years older than he and had been married before, worked as an accountant.

While I was studying at university, I became interested in Kung-Fu and I joined a martial arts club in London. I was an eager student, but I could not properly assess the quality of the club, or of the training. Then, after a year or so, and as a result of an apparently chance meeting with an acquaintance of the chief instructor, I found my way to a small group of Shaolin Chan Kung-Fu practitioners. During the following years, I worked hard, and was trained according to a schedule that mirrors what has been described in the early part of this book. I also learned a good deal about the Hong Kong school and about the promotion of its principles and practices in the West. Occasionally, visitors from Hong Kong conducted seminars, which were important events for us.

After university, I married, had two children, and made my living as a journalist. Gradually, my career led me to lucrative assignments abroad, sometimes for several months. While I was on one of these extended assignments, I connected with a local Shaolin Chan Kung-Fu group, and in 1980 Philippe visited. He was already a revered figure, referred to simply as 'Dragon Master'. We worked together for several weeks, and, to cut a long story short, he invited me to Hong Kong for an intensive, two-month course – if I could manage it.

As it turned out, I was able to arrange a transfer, and I moved to Hong Kong, with my family, for two years, during which I trained at the Hong Kong school. Subsequently, Philippe and I stayed in touch, meeting regularly though not frequently. Over the years, I came to realise how important for him was the promotion of an authentic Kung-Fu tradition in the West, and, in that context, we talked a good deal about the Second World War, which had been such a formative and unsettling experience for him. I explained that during those years, my father had an influential position in the Foreign Office. I had learned from him about the Japanese defeat in the Pacific, and about the chaos in Hong Kong afterwards. He also told me that fears about Russia invading Japan had precipitated the decision to drop the atomic bombs. If Japan surrendered quickly, there would be no need to deal with Russia in a post-war settlement. My father had no love for Russia, and was a vehement cold warrior. I remember Philippe remarking, then, quietly, "We all have our stories." But now I find myself wondering about my own story, which has been interwoven for such a long time with his. Did he perhaps want me to know more, to find out more, to look further? And so I find myself entertaining the ghost of a possibility – outlandish, far-fetched, an ignis fatuus flickering, yet persistent, in the recesses of my mind.

I had not been able to discover anything about my mother's first marriage, except that it wasn't talked about, and the reasons had something to do with the Foreign Office and the cold war. But the dates work out. Could it be? Could there perhaps be a half-sister? Could Philippe after all not let go of her entirely? Or was he trying to help me out by leading me to something I would find important to know, if I chose? Or was there any plan at all? As he said, we all have our stories. But now that I see what I have just written, in cold print, I tell myself that, everything considered, such a story really, indeed, would not be likely.